Ilse Kaufmann and Helena Pardo

THE JOURNEY OF ILSE KAUFMANN
Vienna–Prague–Buenos Aires

Ilse Kaufmann and Helena Pardo

THE JOURNEY OF ILSE KAUFMANN

Vienna–Prague–Buenos Aires

Translated from the Spanish by Susana Urra

Yad Vashem ⋆ Jerusalem
The International Institute for Holocaust Research

Ilse Kaufmann and Helena Pardo
La Historia de Ilse

Academic Editor: Avraham Milgram
Language & Production Editor: Gayle Green

Responsibility for the opinions expressed in this publication is solely that of the authors.

P.O. Box 3477, Jerusalem 9103401, Israel
publications.marketing@yadvashem.org.il
First published in Spanish by Emecé Editores, 2002

ISBN 978-965-308-475-9

Typesetting: Judith Sternberg
Printed in Israel by the State of Israel Government Printer, Jerusalem

This book is dedicated to the memory of my husband Bela and my son Carlos; to Carlos' children, my grandchildren; to my daughter Lizy and her children, Andrea and Alex; and to the memory of my parents Paul Hahn and Karoline Goldschmidt.

This book would not exist had it not been for the good soul who encouraged me to tell my story. My warmest thanks go to Helena Pardo for sharing my journey through life with a dedication beyond measure.

– Ilse Kaufmann

To Marga Kupferminc de Indij, a true friend; Juan, my husband and best friend; and to whom I owe everything, my three children, María Graciela, Juan and María Marta, with heartfelt love.

– Helena Pardo

CONTENTS

FOREWORD

The story of Ilse Kaufmann, which is told in the first person, is not the result of a monologue but of a long conversation that she and I had over the course of 15 months. We met at her house once a week – almost always on Thursday afternoons – with something akin to religious discipline. During our meetings she slowly told me the story of her life, while I asked questions and made comments that helped bring her more remote feelings and memories, or those that her subconscious guarded more closely, to the surface.

Our long dialogue began the first time we met, on September 3, 1998. I started writing the book two weeks later, after listening to the recordings and reading the notes that Ilse had made throughout the years so she wouldn't forget dates and events, for she had long harbored the notion of leaving a written testimony of her life.

Our working dialogue ended on June 25, 2000, when we considered the book to be complete. However, our dialogue as friends continues to this day, and I must admit that I often feel tempted to add something to this book, because there is so much left to say. During this working period, which was twice interrupted by our respective summer breaks and the occasional rest for health reasons, Ilse's story slowly began to take shape, while at the same time a solid friendship emerged between us.

Before embarking on this project, she and I agreed that everything in the book would be rigorously true – and this responsibility fell to Ilse alone, since

I neither witnessed nor experienced the events that I describe for her – and we also agreed that we would both be the book's coauthors. Trusting her words entirely, I started listening, organizing and writing.

But when did all this really begin? It might have been one day in 1982 when Juan and I boarded a plane to go and visit the State of Israel and learn about its capacity for building methods; or perhaps, when feeling motivated by everything I had seen there, I decided to learn Hebrew as a deep-felt personal tribute to the Jewish people, who were building their own country and achieving true miracles, such as making life spring up in the desert. Maybe that is where the seed was sown, because when I returned to Buenos Aires I enrolled in a Hebrew course at the Argentine-Israeli Cultural Exchange Institute, and there I met Marga Kupferminc, who has remained a true friend during all the years that have elapsed since then, as have our families. After studying the language for seven years and graduating together, we both held private conversation sessions – sometimes at her house, sometimes at mine – and our friendship was cemented during those years.

It was Marga who told Ilse Kaufmann that I could write her biography. Marga, who had met Ilse at her sister Mirta's art workshop, knew that I would do it. She was quite sure of it seeing that she knows me so well.

Ilse needed someone to write the book for her in Spanish, because her grandchildren Andrea and Alex Swiec Kaufmann, who live in Madrid, had often asked her to leave a written testimony of her life, which was marked by a succession of curious events, sad memories, long periods of fear and hardship and a constant fight for survival. She had had to struggle to rebuild everything that had been lost during, and because of, the war. Ilse told stories to her grandchildren every time they met, but they were not satisfied with mere words and demanded that she write this book.

I would rather not go into too much detail on how we came to meet – Ilse talks about it at the end of her story – although I feel that a whole other book could be written on the subject, with Ilse's daughter Lizy and Mirta Kupferminc and her paintings as the main characters.

For now, I will simply dedicate a paragraph to Ilse Kaufmann's remarkably good memory. She never mentioned a historical fact or date that was wrong and I really must stress that all the information she gave me was always consistent with what I found in encyclopedias or the various histories of World War II that I keep in my personal library. She also managed her endless "deposit" of photographs and documents with amazing precision, never once losing her vitality and enthusiasm despite several health problems during the preparation of this book.

And so here it is, finally, the story of Ilse Kaufmann, a woman who fought not only for her own life but also for the life of her loved ones; a woman who had the people she most loved taken from her by Death, and who will always carry in her heart the indelible and harrowing pain of losing her son Carlos – the worst kind of sorrow a human being can experience. I have written the story with constant interest and occasional horror, and always with respect. I have come close to a cruel war that I was lucky enough not to experience personally, but I have felt as my own the anguish, the fear, the hunger and the grief of those who did. I have also felt the blessing of peace, in whose kingdom anything is possible. And during the course of this story, I made a friend whose name is Ilse. Edith Ilse. Ilse Kaufmann.

– Helena Pardo

PREFACE

The Second World War was a decisive moment in history. We all remember the names of the dictators, heads of government, generals and other great characters who shaped this period of history. However, often amongst the big names and dates, the stories of ordinary people and how their lives were affected by war is lost, but the truth is that these stories are important and deserve to be remembered. My grandmother, like many others at the time, had to suffer the inhumanity and insanity of a war in which the worst human values seemed to have no limits. This book is her testimony to the history of the Second World War and her life during that time.

This is the story of a Jewish family, my family, who went from being one of the most important families in Vienna to having barely enough to eat. It's the story of a woman who had to fight to survive in order to save her loved ones. It is a story of distress, hope and second chances in a new, distant and unknown country. I am sure you will find the story – written by Helena Pardo and lived by my grandmother – entertaining, exciting and full of deep learning insights. However, we must not forget that it is a true story, told by a real person, with implications on her life and the lives of her loved ones.

My grandmother never told us about that time of her life during the war. She spoke of her life in Argentina, a land of peace and tranquility, leaving the pain in the past, in order to make space for happy moments with loved ones in the present. But the reality is that the woman who made traditional Austrian desserts for us and spoke in German with my mother on the phone was the same woman who shared the story of her life with Helena Pardo. She is the same woman who looked after us during our visits to Buenos Aires, the woman who shared the last years of her life with us in Madrid, and the woman who lived the life narrated in this book.

I have had to go through the exercise of understanding that this novel is the story of my grandmother. It has been through her story and her legacy that I have learned some important life lessons, which, to this day, I always adhere to.

First, she made me very aware of the injustices that still exist in the world and I now see that behind the current war headlines and important names, there are also people who, like my grandmother in the past, are suffering great injustices. I understand that the items we see on television and read in the papers related to war should not be foreign to us. It is our duty as human beings to become more aware of the suffering taking place inside war zones and do whatever is possible to stop it.

Second, she taught me through her life and her story that even in the darkest moments of history there are people who fight injustice and give aid without asking for anything in return. Even in moments of total despair, there is also hope and we must never give up and must keep fighting for a better future.

I hope you enjoy reading this great story, that you can draw some useful lessons from it, that you become more aware of the suffering that is inflicted on people in war zones, and that you still have hope for human kindness – even in your darkest moments.

– Alex Swiec Kaufmann

PART ONE

EUROPE

ILSE

My name is Ilse, Edith Ilse. My last name is Hahn by birth and Kaufmann by marriage. For a long time now, everyone has been calling me Ilse Kaufmann. That's right, I am now Ilse Kaufmann, that same woman who was born in Vienna after World War I.

But am I really the same woman? I have wondered about it so often! So many things have happened since then; there has been so much pain; so many injustices have been committed; death has haunted my life so often! I have asked myself this question many, many times. And every time I searched for an answer, I ended up convincing myself — imposing on myself, forcing myself to accept — that the only answer that feels good, the only one that has helped me, and continues to help me get through life is, yes; I am indeed that same woman who was born in Vienna after World War I, born into a nurturing home where peace, safety, comfort and a good life were the norm.

And that is why I am telling this story, the story of my life, the story of Ilse Kaufmann: to find support in it, to extract strength and hope from the memories of hardship that was overcome through self-sacrifice, sharp wit, cunning, or simply the will to live. I am doing it for my grandchildren, so they will know where they came from and why they are here in this world. And I am telling them this story so that, aware that they are the offspring of survivors, they will strive to turn this world into a kingdom of justice, peace and love for themselves and for those to come, and as a tribute to those who never even had the chance to be born, because the flower was picked before bearing the fruit that contained the seed of life.

When I was born on November 7, 1920, my father was 26 years old and my mother was 24. I was an only child. My father was a Viennese banker who knew how to manage his assets, but he gave his family more than just a good material life: He also thought of himself as a *paterfamilias* and actively exercised his fatherhood – which focused entirely on me – by protecting me, cuddling me as much as was healthy for a child, demanding that I behave in accordance with our intellectual and social position in society, and instilling in me the moral and ethical values he had learned from his elders, and which he himself always lived by.

I loved my father. I loved him more than I loved my mother. His name was Paul Hahn. As I already said, he was a banker, but I should also add that he was one of the ten most important bankers in Vienna. I know he did business with high-ranking people. Around 1926 he carried out financial operations for the Belgian monarchy and was summoned to Belgium by the king himself. I was only six at the time, so I found out about it years later, as a teenager, when these professional successes still echoed at the friends' reunions and social gatherings at our house.

My mother, Karoline Goldschmidt, was a very beautiful woman. Of average height, she had a very good figure and chestnut-colored hair, and was admired by all. She was extremely fussy about her appearance and devoted her entire time to it, displaying little interest in domestic affairs and always preferring to delegate responsibilities. She was also not very fond of playing with me when I was little – and I confess I would have very much liked her to share some of my games. I don't want to be unfair to her, but if I am telling the story of my life, then I want to tell it from my own point of view, in all sincerity and good faith.

My mother was the great-granddaughter of a Rothschild who married a Goldschmidt; they had several children, including a daughter, Fanny, who also married a Goldschmidt. That union produced eight children, one of whom was Mathilde, my mother's mother, who also married a Goldschmidt, although this particular one was Czech and not German like the others, who all hailed from Frankfurt. My Grandmother Mathilde was afflicted by a great sorrow that may well have had something to do with the licentiousness of my grandfather Wilhelm, an intelligent man with good looks and an interest in science. Mathilde was treated by Sigmund Freud at a time when psychoanalysis was taking its first steps.

I don't remember my grandfather Wilhelm Goldschmidt because he died when I was two years old, but I do know that he was interested in astronomy and that he had an impressive library where one could find a wealth of information about this branch of science, which fascinated him to the point that he owned several telescopes to observe the skies and the movement of the stars. I know that once, when there was an eclipse of the sun, he traveled to Madrid because that was the best location from which to see it.

My Grandmother Mathilde died at the concentration camp in Auschwitz. I still have the last two letters she wrote to me, one sent from Olmütz[1] on July 4, 1942 – before being deported to Theresienstadt[2] – and the other without a date, but bearing a post office stamp from July 31 of the same year, right before being deported to Auschwitz. The texts of both letters are included later in this book.

On my father's side, I mostly remember my Grandmother Sophia Meyer, my father's mother, who died at age 59 of a heart condition for which she was treated at a clinic in Mayerling, near Baden. Nobody bothered to tell my father about her admission to, and agony at, the clinic – he was simply informed of her death. This prompted my father to file a serious and moving complaint with the clinic authorities, who deprived him of the chance to be with his dear mother during those final moments. My father loved his mother dearly, and he inspired in her a sense of motherly love and protection that was inverted years later, when he strove to always keep her from harm. I knew my paternal grandfather, Joseph Hahn, only through what other people told me about him, because he died suddenly in Teplitz Schönau,[3] the small town where he was born, when my father was only two years old.

1 Today, Olomouc.

2 Theresienstadt was a ghetto and transit camp for Jews expelled from Bohemia and Moravia, Germany, The Netherlands, Denmark and more than a thousand children from the Białystok Ghetto. Most of them, after staying short or long periods, were deported to death camps including Auschwitz-Birkenau.

3 After World War I, Teplice-Šanov became part of the newly established Czechoslovakia. Teplice was annexed by Nazi Germany according to the 1938 Munich Agreement. After World War II the Czechoslovak government enacted the Beneš decrees, after which the

Sophia Meyer and Joseph Hahn, my paternal grandparents, had four children. The eldest, Ernesto, never married, rarely worked, was a dedicated gambler – he adored Monte Carlo – and gave his family many headaches. Grette, the second child, married a man named Kaiser and didn't have any children. The third child was Gertrude, who died of cancer at age 34, three days after the Nazis occupied Vienna. She and her husband, whose family name was Elias, had a son named Robert, who is my only surviving relative following the horror of the concentration camps where almost all the others perished. Robert Elias, my first cousin, currently lives in London, often travels "in search of the sun," and I have met up with him on several occasions in various parts of the world. Not long ago, he came to see me in Buenos Aires and as we sat there reflecting on the old days we agreed that even though we both had happy childhoods, the Nazis stole our adolescence and forced us into a bitter, premature adulthood. The fourth child of my grandparents was Paul, my father, whose education was overseen by his grandfather Edward Hahn after being left fatherless at an early age.

The Hahn family came from Sudetenland, the tough mountain region on the northern, southwest, and western border areas of Czechoslovakia, and which now sets the limit between the Czech Republic, Germany, Austria and Poland. My father inherited the character of the people who inhabit this land, which explains his marked austerity and inflexible rectitude.

We lived in a residential neighborhood in Vienna, on Wiederhofergasse 8, in the Ninth District. Ours was a very large apartment full of elegant furniture and rich ornaments, many of which were made of porcelain, silver and crystal. We Central Europeans really appreciate crystal, and I still have a tendency to use good crystal to decorate my home. I am seduced by its sparkle, its transparent sharpness, and the play of light that is multiplied by each of its sharp, glimmering cuts.

I was educated in Vienna. For the first two years I went to a state school, then switched to a private *gymnasium*, the equivalent of high school in Argentina. I never finished *gymnasium* as a regular student; instead, when I still had a year to go, I took an examination and obtained the final diploma. I was a good student, everything seemed easy to me, which resulted in

"ethnic German" population was expelled from Teplice, located in northwestern Bohemia near the border with the German state of Saxony.

occasional boredom in class. In order to complete my education I enrolled in university and attended an art history course. I was very interested in art, so I truly enjoyed this course.

Of all the arts, theater is what I was most interested in, but my father would not hear of my studying this subject. When I was 14, my *fräulein* Berta no longer walked me to school and one day after class I decided to go to the Grosser Konzerthaussaal, where the Academy of Performing Arts was housed. When I got there I spoke with Professor Henry von Perrfall, who made me deliver some lines to see what I could do. I selected a passage from *Faust* in which a pregnant Gretchen prays to the Virgin Mary as she intones a poignant *mea culpa*: "*Ach neige, du Schmerzensreiche, Dein Antlitz gnädig meiner Not!*" (Oh Bend Thou, Mother of Sorrows, Send Thou a Look of Pity on My Pain!). My performance caused a more than favorable impression, and I enthusiastically told von Perrfall that I wanted to sign up for classes at the academy. However, he would not let me do so without my parents' consent, so I talked my mother into coming with me and helping me enroll. My first two years at the academy were highly successful, but in the middle of the third, war broke out, effectively interrupting my career. It was a great personal loss and my theatrical calling was cut short forever.

My *gymnasium* studies also provided me with a religious education. Once a week we had two hours of religion class, when we were divided into two groups: The Jewish students had a teacher who taught us the most relevant issues of our creed – the history of the Jewish people, the Bible, the Hebrew language, prayers, traditions and so on – while a priest taught the essentials of Christianity to the Catholic students, who made up the largest group. Our teacher was a mean, sour woman and none of us liked her. One day I smeared soap on the floor to make her slip and fall…and she did! It was one of my many school pranks, which the other students always celebrated with great glee.

I was a mischievous, happy child who lived in a cushioned nest, and I retained that joyful spirit for many years despite the horrors of war. It was the death of my son Carlos that drove the joy from my heart and erased the smile from my lips. I will talk about this tremendous misfortune in due time.

Another one of my pranks involved throwing one of the principal's snow boots out the window on one of the several occasions when I was called into her office. When she realized what had happened, she stormed into our classroom and exclaimed: "Hahn did this, no doubt!" And there was no doubt that I had.

But one day I did something worse that resulted in a serious rebuke from the school authorities and which incensed my father when he found out.

It so happened that all my schoolmates had beautiful boxes of coloring pencils made by the Swiss company Staedtler. They, like me, came from wealthy families, but my father had experienced the rigors of life from an early age after my grandfather died young, and he imposed an austere education on me that was rather excessive and in sharp contrast with the spirit of largesse with which our home was run. This unshakeable attitude of his when it came to the possession of certain material goods was the reason I did not have those coloring pencils that so dazzled me and for which I pined.

That box of 12 Staedtler coloring pencils kept me awake at night. My father insisted that I was still too young — I must have been about eight years old at the time — to handle such a collection of "nearly professional" tools and he yielded neither to my pleas, nor to my tears. Finally, like someone who knows that a battle is lost but the war is not over, I decided to solve the problem on my own.

The Goldschmidts from Horice (Czechoslovakia) with their children.
Standing: Wilhelm Goldschmidt, Ilse's grandfather (wearing a military uniform) and Olilie Goldschmidt (who later married a Ruhman).
Sitting: One of the Goldschmidt siblings; the Goldschmidts (Ilse's great-grandparents) and Luzi Goldschmidt (who later married a Friedländer).

I noticed that my classmates left their school things on their desks when they went out for recess and after several days of close observation, I drew up a plan of action and implemented it straight away. I told my teacher that I was not feeling well and would rather stay inside instead of going out to the playground. Permission was granted, and when I was alone inside the classroom I grabbed a girl's box of pencils – she always left it on her desk, as I had duly noted during my sleuthing activities – and threw it into the garbage. During the next recess, I was again alone in class and, with a clear conscience, I took the box of pencils "that was in the garbage," as I told myself, and slipped it

Joseph Hahn and Sophia Meyer, Ilse's paternal grandparents, on their wedding day.

Ilse's maternal grandmother, Mathilde Goldschmidt, in her wedding gown at the height of her youth.

inside my briefcase. I had not stolen the pencils, I had simply found them lying in the garbage. When I returned home from school that day and Berta went through my things as usual, she found the box of pencils. I was subjected to an exhausting interrogation and the next day, Berta went to see the principal and asked if any of the girls had reported something missing. The answer, of course, was affirmative: A box of Staedtler coloring pencils had disappeared.

All this information was swiftly and faithfully conveyed to my father, who flew into a rage and went to talk to the school authorities. They all agreed to suspend me for seven days – after returning the beloved pencils to their rightful owner – and when we returned home my father placed me on his knees and spanked my soft, pink bottom so conscientiously that I had to sleep on my side for several days. While he was spanking me, he kept repeating that he would rather have a dead daughter than a thieving daughter. Many years later, when I was already living in Argentina, I happened to travel through Switzerland and bought myself a box of Staedtler coloring pencils that I still treasure and have never shared with anybody. This is a clue as to the kind of "affective-emotional" trauma that I suffered as an eight-year-old because I did not own a simple box of 12 Staedtler coloring pencils.

Ilse's father, Paul Hahn, and his sisters Grette and Gertrude. Gertrude died of cancer three days after the Nazis occupied Vienna. Not pictured here is their older brother Ernesto, who loved gambling and Monte Carlo.

THE SUMMER HOUSE

We spent the warm months of July and August at our summer house some 35 kilometers from Vienna, in Bad Vöslau,[4] near Mayerling. The house, located on Hügelgasse 32, went by the romantic name of the Veilchen Villa, meaning "Violet Villa." I enjoyed living in that bright, spacious house whose ground floor held a hall, a music room and a dining room with service areas, while the upper floor had five bedrooms, two bathrooms, one terrace out front and a covered one at the back. There was a garden running all around it and a house for the servants to one side. It was equipped as though it were a city house, ready to be lived in all year round. I remember that during the summer vacation the rugs from our apartment in Vienna were taken to the summer house and beaten with wicker canes to remove the dirt – there were no vacuum cleaners back then. One day, I counted 38 Persian rugs that were taken to Vöslau for cleaning on a horse-drawn carriage that took 12 hours to get there, although the journey probably included some time out for the driver to comfort himself with lunch, an afternoon snack and a bit of wine.

We owned an electromobile, a type of battery-powered vehicle from the 1920s in which the driver traveled in a kind of high coachman's seat. These automobiles had been developed in France in 1889, but ours was a German model, a 1922 Horch. Besides this vehicle, which would nowadays be described as environmentally friendly because it had no toxic emissions, we also had two regular Steyr cars that were driven by Tuman, our chauffeur. Yes, I enjoyed living at the summer house. I enjoyed the heat, the sun, the country air, the plants, the flowers...the holidays!

It was precisely during those summer months that my *fraülein* Berta – who practically raised me and who was always by my side until I left Europe for Argentina – taught me how to keep a home and practical things such as cooking, baking, washing clothes or setting up a clothesline in the yard. My domestic abilities were greatly improved through this kind of training, which Bella's nature regarded as necessary and which she strove to convey to me. So many times I was forced to perform chores while my friends were out skating or enjoying a game of tennis.... My maternal grandmother was opposed to this type of practical education and she always told Berta: "My granddaughter will

4 Bad Vöslau is a spa town in Lower Austria.

never have to do this kind of work! She will always have someone to wait on her!" To which my governess would invariably reply, "Neither you nor anyone else knows what the future will bring. She needs to learn everything. She might need it one day!" Berta was not mistaken. Time would prove her right. And that is how my childhood elapsed in what I like to define as a "bed of roses."

Ilse's parents, Paul Hahn and Karoline Goldschmidt, at Veilchen Villa.
At her feet sits Putzi, the little dog that Alicia Heller (Aunt Alicia) refers to in her last letter before being deported to Theresienstadt.

Veilchen Villa, the summer house that Ilse's parents owned in Bad Vöslau, near Mayerling. This is the way it looked before the war, before the terrace was built over the front door.

BERTA

The great love I professed for my father neutralized the effect caused by the blend of coldness and indifference that I sensed in my mother, and which I still perceive to this day – even though, like I said earlier, I do not want to be unfair to her. Sometimes our perception of an event or an attitude is diametrically opposed to the real intentions behind it. Despite what it might seem, my father's firm character, his excessive austerity and his rigorous methods, far from bothering me or inhibiting me, made me view him as a man of great moral fortitude – someone who made me feel completely safe and in possession of an indestructible happiness. He was the solid rock against which I could lean and feel protected.

In that delightful setting of my childhood days, my governess Berta, my *fräulein*, played a very important role. Berta was the woman who loved me as

Berta Pietsch, Ilse's *fräulein*, who was with her at all times until she left for Argentina.

one loves a daughter, and who always took care of me, not just as a child but during the entire time I spent in Europe. Berta neglected herself in order to be with me and educate me, and disregarded the possibility of having a family of her own, since all her time, energy and her life were spent on me. This woman had started working as a maid in our home before I was born. An unforgivable mistake by my first governess, whom my father found sleeping one night instead of tending to my relentless crying, caused her to be summarily dismissed and replaced by Berta.

Berta was born on August 29, 1894 in Böhmisch-Leipa,[5] in the Sudetenland, and her entire temperament faithfully reflected her tough origins. I have already talked about her demanding training sessions, her unflagging devotion, her vision and her premonitions about what my future might hold in store. She was strict and harsh, but also incredibly good, especially to me.

I could not have done all the things I did when the scourge of Nazism descended on the European Jews, plunging us all into the darkest and most inhuman night of mankind, if Berta had not tempered my character as a child, taught me how to do housework, and shown me how to keep my feet on the ground thanks to her practical sense and wise judgment. In some ways, I am the way I am because of my father, but in many other ways — perhaps the more practical ones — I owe it to Berta that I was able to survive the cruel change of lifestyle imposed by the war. Berta forced me to learn all kinds of housework as well as home economics, so that when we were forced to live "on nothing," it was I who solved all our problems thanks to her wise and far-sighted lessons. When we were forced to leave our belongings behind in our flight from Nazi horror, Berta kept many of our things for us and returned them after the war. These items included photographs, letters and documents, as well as paintings and other ornaments that were important to us not just for their monetary worth but also for their sentimental value.

I parted ways with Berta when we managed to escape from Prague to Spain. It was a miracle that she had been by my side all that time, even on the days prior to the birth of my son, and that she was there to help me care for the newborn and assist me in my struggle to get away from that bloody war and the horrors of extermination, to which we were doomed as Jews. I saw her again in 1962, when my daughter Alicia (Lizy) was 12 years old and we traveled to

5 Today, Česká Lípa.

Prague together so the two could meet – and also so Alicia could meet her paternal Aunt Clara Kaufmann, an Auschwitz survivor, whom I will talk about when the Kaufmanns come into the story of my life.

Berta was a Christian and came from a family of confirmed Nazis. She did not share her family's political views; in fact, her own ideas were quite different, as her actions later proved. As far as religion goes, I must emphasize that it was never an obstacle in our relationship, but rather a reason for mutual respect. When the war ended, Czechoslovakia came under Communist rule and Berta, who by then was living with a good family in Haida,[6] in the Sudetenland, ran the risk of being considered a Nazi and deported to Germany. My husband, who worked for the Argentine Republic's diplomatic representation in Czechoslovakia, sent the authorities a note, bearing an official seal, stating that Berta was not a Nazi, that she had always helped Jews, and asking for special permission to allow her to remain in her homeland.

Until the day she died, Berta received the equivalent of 200 US dollars every month from my husband in Buenos Aires, which helped her live in better conditions. When Berta died in Haida in 1970, her niece told us that she had had a dignified death and burial, and that before passing away she had asked for a photograph to be placed under the pillow of her coffin. It was a photograph of someone who was not her daughter by blood but was certainly her daughter in her heart: Ilse Hahn. I also loved her very much and she knew it. Her memory is always with me, and I pray that my feelings of eternal gratitude and tenderness will reach her, wherever she is.

A TURN FOR THE WORSE

The political situation in Austria had become increasingly unstable in the years of growing political and social unrest in Europe after World War I – a conflict with such complex and confusing consequences that it created even worse problems than the original ones, and exacerbated unresolved feelings of resentment and hatred to the point of unmanageability. Instead of blue skies, the postwar period created a clash of lightning that was the forerun-

6 Today, Nový Bor.

ner of that other great storm, World War II, which was infinitely crueler and unfathomably worse.

The climate was one of increasing uncertainty and apprehension since the assassination of Chancellor Engelbert Dollfuss[7] on July 25, 1934. On that day, black crepe hung from all the windows in Vienna, and at night many candles were lit with the fire of indignation and pain caused by his death. The murder did not quite create a climate of outright antisemitism, but it was obvious that something was changing, and not exactly for the better. We listened to the news on the radio with a blend of anxiety and distress caused by our collective sense of foreboding. We tried to lead normal lives, but our attitude was less and less spontaneous because fear had begun to cast a shadow over us.

THE LAST NIGHT OF 1937

I had been invited to a party at a friend's house not far from ours on the last day of 1937. It was an intensely cold, clear night and the brightness made the sky seem bluer and the stars twinkle with a crystalline light. Because of a recent heavy snowfall, we thought it would be better to walk than drive and my parents decided to walk with me. Together, we covered the distance to my friend's house in near-silent wonderment, grateful for this privilege that God was placing before our eyes – this landscape of snow, starry skies and intense cold that turned our breath into clouds of mist, which filtered out of our mouths and through our scarves. All the elements seemed to play off each other and come together in harmonious unity, resulting in a magic that was at once cause and effect. We walked quietly, with a light step, our gloved hands holding each other tight, our hearts beating fast. It was a magical moment, unforgettable and sublime. A deep, majestic silence surrounded and contained us, and we inhabited this silence, enjoying the sheer pleasure of it. It was the last night of the year, and this was undoubtedly a rite of revelation. There was

7 In early 1933, he shut down parliament, banned the Austrian Nazi party and assumed dictatorial powers. Suppressing the Socialist movement in February 1934, he cemented the rule of "austrofascism" through the authoritarian First of May Constitution. Dollfuss was assassinated as part of a failed coup attempt by Nazi agents in 1934. His successor, Dr. Kurt von Schuschnigg, maintained his regime until Adolf Hitler's annexing of Austria in 1938.

so much greatness in that magic! There was so much mystery in that beauty! I was 17 and I was happy. We gripped each other's hands more tightly and when I think back on that scene I still hear the light crunch of our footsteps on the snow and the strong beating of my heart.

I barely remember my friend's party, but I will never forget that last night of 1937. It was the last New Year's Eve we would ever spend in Vienna. Three months later, the tragedy began.

AUNT ALICIA

On March 5, 1938, I traveled to Olmütz, a small town in Moravia near Brno, the capital of that Czechoslovak region. Olmütz, or Olomouc in Czech, had become part of Czechoslovakia in 1918 and besides being a refined, aristocratic old city, it was also – and predominantly – an intellectual center that was home to Palacký University, named after František Palacký, the distinguished nineteenth century Czech historian who wrote *The History of the Czech Nation in Bohemia and Moravia*, a markedly nationalist book that would take him into politics. Awash with churches and ancient palaces, Olmütz has a history going back to 1063, when it became the seat of a bishopric. It was the capital of Moravia before Brno, until 1640, and it was also the city where Emperor Ferdinand I of Austria abdicated in favor of his nephew Franz Joseph on December 2, 1848.

I had been invited to a *Purim* dance in Olmütz and was to stay at Bismarckstrasse 7, the house of my Aunt Alicia, who was my mother's younger (and only) sister. An immensely wealthy woman, she was the widow of Marko Heller, one of the owners of the Pilsen breweries and also the owner of the Opp chocolate and Libo candy factories. When my Uncle Marko Heller died of a brain tumor at age 50, his beautiful and beloved wife Alicia was only 32. They had no children but loved their three nieces as if they were their own. I was one of those nieces; the other two were the daughters of Marko's sister, Josephine Friedmann. I was by far the youngest of the three: Liese was 17 years my elder, and Gerty was ten years older than I was. Marko's will stated that upon his death, each of his three nieces would receive the equivalent of 100,000 of today's dollars on their wedding day.

Aunt Alicia used to play with me when I was little, and once we both decorated a two-storey doll's house that I was crazy about, fitting it with lights and lots of decorations. We would also dress up my dolls together, pretend to visit one another, and she would read me stories and pamper me.

I remember the excitement I felt over this trip – the endless preparations, picking out the right luggage among the many suitcases we had at home, selecting the outfit I would wear, thinking about the party itself. It was the excitement of a 17-year-old girl who fantasized that a manly arm would clasp her waist during the dance, making her heart quicken as they waltzed across the floor together. I dreamed about the possibility of romance and imagined Prince Charming standing there before me.

My mother and I decided that I would wear an aqua green tulle dress that I had recently worn for the first time at a graduation party in Vienna. It was truly lovely, and not unlike those worn by the Empress Sisi. My hairdo would also imitate the way she styled her hair when she showed herself in public with those generous cleavages that she made famous, and I was to have a curly strand of hair hanging down from a small bunch of flowers on the side of my head. The entire household was attuned to the intense joy that I felt in the days before the journey. Sometimes my excitement would take the shape of lengthy discussions on how this or that music should be danced to, while other times it turned into nervous strain, making me burst into laughter or tears for no particular reason. At times, I would have long conversations with friends, who by turns burned with enthusiasm or seethed with envy. In short, there was no mistaking the festive atmosphere that reigned around me.

The day of departure arrived and my parents took me to the station. Aunt Alicia, whom I loved so much, would be waiting for me in Olmütz, and on the day of the dance, there really was a Prince Charming.

THE DANCE

That *Purim* dance was an unforgettable event for me with all the guests richly dressed and a pervasive mood of cheerfulness all around. Soon after I arrived, a dashing young man in a military uniform invited me to dance, and I immediately felt there was something special about this meeting. As we twirled to the beat of the waltz, the dreams I had woven since the moment I received the invitation suddenly seemed to be coming true. I was

Ilse at age 15. This is the picture she sent her husband's father before her wedding.

fascinated by this young man and flirted happily, showing off my pretty dress and Viennese accent, and letting my curls fall graciously on my bare shoulder. When the dance was over, other young men took me out on the dance floor, but that vibration, that feeling that "a real encounter" had taken place, did not occur again. The dashing young military man did not come back for me, but at least I'd had the thrill of dancing with my prince.

I danced a lot and had great fun that night; I felt pampered and courted by everyone who knew I was the niece of the young, beautiful, wealthy widow Alicia Heller, who enjoyed a very good reputation in Olmütz's social circles. Even though outside our doors a fire was being kindled in Europe, inside that *Purim* dance hall, nothing hinted at the fact that we were just one step away from horror.

The following morning we got up later than usual, as is bound to happen after a party. My aunt and I had breakfast together and delighted in a detailed review of the previous evening's highlights, including the good music, the women's elegant dresses, their luxurious jewels and the men's impeccable attire. The comments continued throughout lunch, teatime and dinner, growing in scope as our memories became laced with a good dose of fantasy and some naughtiness as well.

Now that we no longer had to prepare for the dance, my aunt and I began going out together every day. Around sunset, we would take a walk in Olmütz square, a ritual that used to be observed in all provincial towns. This traditional evening stroll was also a genteel rendezvous for young people to weave and unweave countless romances and courtships. The not-so-young participated in this ritual too, with the men sitting on either side of the path as the women strolled back and forth, flirting when they noticed themselves being observed, greeted or smiled at.

At that particular time there was a violet seller who sold those classic little bunches of blue scented violets trimmed with dark green leaves. Every evening, the violet seller would hand me a bouquet, courtesy of someone whose name she never told me, but who, I hoped, was the dashing young man in the military uniform who had waltzed with me at the *Purim* dance. But the man's identity remained a mystery, and every night before going to bed I would look at my violets and dream about Prince Charming.

A BIT OF HISTORY

On Friday, March 11, 1938, Austria's chancellor, Dr. Kurt von Schuschnigg – successor to Chancellor Engelbert Dollfuss, who had been assassinated on July 25, 1934 – addressed the Austrian people to say goodbye, just like the German field marshal and statesman Paul von Hindenburg had done with his own people in 1932 when, easily convinced by von Papen and big industrial interests, he offered Hitler the German chancellorship, thus ending his own political leadership and paving the way for the cruel Nazi regime. I remember that day in late 1932 – I was 12 – when we heard the words with which von Hindenburg announced his resignation.[8] A heavy preoccupation invaded our home, as it did thousands of other homes – especially Jewish ones – not just in Germany but also in Austria, Czechoslovakia, Hungary and Poland.

And so, on January 30, 1933, Hitler managed to become the Chancellor of Germany. From that moment on, his unrestrained ambition would know no bounds. Proclaiming himself *Reichsführer*, his Third Reich implemented an incredibly aggressive policy of boundless expansion and he mercilessly eliminated any political, ideological or racial adversaries who stood in his way. Hitler's terror machine would continue to sow death and horror during those 12 long and ill-fated years that I call "the darkest night in the history of humanity," a period marked by the cruelest massacres and the most undignified, inexplicable, unjustifiable and terrifying kind of extermination.

It is not my intention to become a World War II historian; I am merely telling the story of my life, and like I said at the beginning, I am doing it as a legacy to my grandchildren. That is the reason I consider it appropriate and necessary to place events in their historical context, which my grandchildren obviously did not experience themselves. That is the purpose of these brief, explanatory comments.

In his moving farewell address on March 11, 1938, Dr. Schuschnigg spoke these anguished words to the Austrian people: "*Ich weiche der Gewalt*" (I yield before violence). The next day, Nazi troops marched into Austria with their weapons and munitions and their baggage of inhuman cruelty. From that day on and for a long time to come, what had only been a prolonged and nightmarish sense of foreboding, intuited danger and imagined evil started to become a reality. Though widely expected, the news caused a stir throughout the world, and even though it is hard to believe, Austrians actually welcomed the German troops with cheers and applause, especially in Vienna. In our own circle, however, this military occupation had tragic overtones. Fear gripped the Jews; rivers of tears were shed, hearts beat to the point of nearly bursting, throats constricted with anxiety, and without saying a word – prudence demanded it – our pressed lips kept a tight lid on the panic we felt, even as our eyes reddened and our hands clenched with the powerlessness and

8 Editorial note: von Hindenburg did not resign from the presidency when he appointed Adolf Hitler as Chancellor of Germany on January 30, 1933.

indignation we felt at the sight of that arrogant, undulating flag with the swastika advancing over our territory, soiling it as it went.

World War II had not been declared yet. The invasion of Poland, the definitive step before all-out war, would take place later, on September 1, 1939, but the Austrian invasion was one of its preambles. In the almot 18 months that elapsed until Friday, September 1 — when, at 4:45 Greenwich Mean Time, the Nazi army initiated the actions that triggered World War II — the lives of all Jews in the German-occupied countries entered a spiral of anxiety, insecurity, persecution and humiliation that the entire world now knows about, but whose magnitude only we are in a position to truly gauge — we who were condemned simply for being the Children of Israel. Even today, the survivors of those dark, interminable days still feel a shiver of fear — true fear — when we think back on all that horror.

A PRELUDE TO PAIN

On March 12, 1938, news of the invasion of Austria was broadcast on the radio and printed in newspapers across the world. When the reports reached Aunt Alicia and me in the small town of Olmütz, Moravia, we felt as though a dark curtain had fallen before our eyes, separating us forever from the joys of the past. At five in the afternoon my father called from Vienna. For a long time, fearing that our telephone lines might be tapped, we had been speaking in code and now, all he said was: "The child must remain there." The surreptitious advance of antisemitism across Europe was there for anyone to see, but those of us who were to be its victims felt it more acutely. When we talked on the phone we never mentioned people's names directly, instead using vague and confusing references to family ties or friendships, such as "We will go to Mathilde's granddaughter's aunt's house." Mathilde was my grandmother, I was the granddaughter, and the aunt was Aunt Alicia.

My father's phone call did not extend much more beyond that sentence, but it sealed my immediate fate: I was to remain at Aunt Alicia's house until further notice. My aunt's immediate future was also determined there and then: She was forced to lodge me not just for longer than she expected, but indeed indefinitely, which had clearly not been in her plans. It also meant that my parents would remain in Vienna for as long as it took them to find a solution to our problems. The family was being split up, and we didn't like it at all. "Are you all right?" my father asked with emotion. "Yes, we're fine. How about you?" I anxiously replied. "We're fine as well." He was barely able to say goodbye. Both our voices cracked and there was only a long, eloquent silence on the line.

A PERIOD OF CHANGE

A new period had begun. News of the Nazi invasion and my father's laconic but significant telephone call had drawn an indelible and unbridgeable line between one stage of our lives and the next. From that moment on, all the good things and happy moments of my life became memories that slipped further away with each passing minute, to the point of seeming almost unreal. I constantly asked myself in silence: "How can I possibly be here, so far away from my parents, without being able to see them or even feel safe enough to communicate with them? How can this house, to which I came so full of joy and hope, now be the setting for so much uncertainty, anxiety and sudden bitterness? How can we have been so happy and hardly been aware of it?"

The reality that was unfurling before our eyes was so different from anything we had previously experienced that when Aunt Alicia and I hugged each other tearfully, feeling united through our common suffering, I also felt that somehow this feeling of distress, this profound bitterness, was a sad omen for us, almost a revelation: She and I, suddenly, had begun to mean something different to each other. We had become two beings who still loved each other but who would sadly behave according to that cruel human condition, the survival instinct. Many times in the subsequent days, without ever confessing it, we took turns displaying petty and selfish behavior that had never before been part of our attitudes. I made a great effort – though not always successfully – not to let myself fall into such vileness, and I am sure that she did the same.

The following days were very disconcerting. It was like starting a new life with different, unfamiliar habits that we thought we could successfully handle, even though we never really did. With the best of intentions, we made an effort to show each other how we could overcome any obstacles that stood in our way. Perhaps it was the alarming news on the radio and in the papers, or the advice she received from friends, or just her own sharp intuition that caused it, but in any event Aunt Alicia immediately took drastic economic measures, cutting down sharply on her expenses out of fear of losing her money, despite her immense fortune. She fired her servants, arguing that she suspected them of being Nazis. Her housekeeper, Vilma Apfel, showed great surprise at her dismissal, and I, too, was surprised at this decision, especially because from that moment on I was put in charge of the household. Aunt Alicia knew that Berta had taught me domestic work, so she decided that in the absence of hired personnel, this was the right time for me to apply the skills I had learned to the care of her own house. I went at it with the best of intentions, but there were so many rooms in the house, so many large rugs, an infinity of furniture and ornaments, doors and windows with glass panes to clean, and on top of that I had to buy food twice a week at a morning market in Olmütz's central square — the same place where I used to go on my evening strolls and had received bunches of violets, fueling dreams of imminent love.

Everything had changed so much: My welcoming aunt had become something of a boss to me; and the place that, until now, had been our strolling quarters was now the market where I had to walk to and from, lugging heavy loads of fruits and vegetables because Aunt Alicia would not pay the tramway fare for me. Meanwhile, the last bunch of violets was no longer in the violet holder in my room, but drying out between the pages of a book that was very significant to me: Goethe's *Faust*, whose passage about Gretchen I had recited in Vienna, where my acting talent had been recognized by Professor Henry von Perrfall at the Academy of Performing Arts. Except for these changes in our personal lives, the situation in Czechoslovakia still appeared to be almost normal, although the mood was one of "wait and see."

We had no news of my parents and this made me very uneasy. I slept poorly even if I slept all night, but sometimes I simply couldn't fall asleep, or else I would wake up with a start in the middle of the night and stay awake until daybreak. Since it was spring, it got light earlier every day and I was unable to go back to sleep after dawn. A progressive feeling of fatigue crept over me. Although it was true that Berta had taught me how to do household chores, I was unaccustomed to doing them, since there had always been enough personnel at my parents' house to do them for me. My life had been that of a rich girl who studied, met with friends, played sports, went to parties and enjoyed being young. Now, I was slowly losing weight and the despair of not knowing how my parents were doing made me feel terrible.

There were moments when Aunt Alicia seemed strained and fearful; at other times she would gather up her strength suddenly – perhaps due to optimistic thoughts or wishful thinking that everything would pass quickly without hurting us – and organize dinners at home for no fewer than eight people. For her it was a real distraction, but for me it was considerable work, for, while she focused on her role of lady of the house, I was in charge of dinner and had to ensure that every last detail was seen to, so that everything would run smoothly; and besides all that, I had to act the part – at least in front of her guests – of the favorite niece of such an elegant lady. This was after preparing the food and later dealing with chores such as washing, drying and putting away the service, glassware, cutlery and the table linen. Besides these occasional obligations caused by my aunt's sporadic outbursts of optimism that temporarily blinded her to the impending dangers, I also had to keep the house properly heated, a task that required going down to the basement where the firewood was stored and carrying it up the stairs to the second floor, where my aunt's rooms were located.

Meanwhile, back in Vienna, my parents were suffering the first abuses by the Nazis. Jews were being insulted, made to sweep the streets, spat on, and, what's worse, their passports were taken away, turning them into virtual prisoners. Communications were tapped, borders were closed – even more so for those people whose identity papers had been confiscated – and prisons were starting to fill up with Jews who would later be transferred to concentration camps. We knew some of these things through the newspaper *Prager Tageblatt* and a few radio stations, especially the BBC and other stations from Allied countries. But we had no news of my parents, either directly or indirectly.

What appeared to be a normal situation in Czechoslovakia was changing day to day due to a whirlwind of suspicious news that gave rise to increasingly well-founded fears. The state of affairs could no longer be described as wait-and-see: With each passing moment we were sinking deeper into a swamp that threatened to swallow us all up. Even though Olmütz was a rich, provincial town, it was quickly losing that serene charm, that elegance that had lent it such a distinguished and aristocratic air. Its peace-loving inhabitants were modifying their daily habits, changing their schedules, losing their kindness, withholding their fresh, spontaneous greetings. A sorrowful gesture was changing their genteel smiles into looks of distrust, and a veil of sadness now tarnished the forthright gaze of their clear Czech eyes. Life at Aunt Alicia's house was also changing faster and faster. The constant rumors were sapping our spirits, because their imprecision sometimes made us exaggerate the dangers around us, while other times we were lulled into a false sense of security when we should have been taking precautions. In any case, the news broadcast on foreign radio stations confirmed that it was necessary to stay alert. Spring wore on and it was no longer so cold, but I was physically exhausted from taking care of the house and I was in a permanent state of stress and anxiety. And even though I didn't show it, I was starting to feel scared. The worst part for me, my real obsession, was not hearing a word from my parents.

While all this was taking place in Czechoslovakia, over in Austria the Nazis had turned into the lords of the land – not just the cities and the picturesque valleys, but also the colorful villages full of gabled-roof houses with balconies of dark, carved wood where thousands of colorful flowers had once brightened the streets and scented the air, while the smoking chimneys gave off the appetizing smell of bread and buns cooking in stoves – a divine smell that its inhabitants would remember for the rest of their lives. Just as with each passing day that I was losing the color on my cheeks, the shine in my eyes and the energy that gave me the strength to carry on, so in Austria everything was fading away: The beauty of its landscape was being marred by the gloomy camouflage colors of the combat tanks; the spontaneous cheerfulness of its people had petered out; and the struggle for survival left no room for the proverbial love of music of the Viennese.

Three long months went by. Summer arrived and it was strange to feel the heat and not be at the Veilchen Villa, our summer home, enjoying the burning midday sun that later made way for the scented evening air. I missed the feeling of renewal that comes from moving to a different place, a different house, where just the thought of the beautiful country garden and the possibility of redecorating my surroundings – even if it was just changing some furniture around or adding small elements to a balcony or terrace – never failed to capture my imagination. Every year, when late May and early June came round, I started feeling the need to pack my bags with sports outfits, light dresses and vaporous muslins for the evenings and the more important social occasions. When the days got longer and hotter, I always needed to feel the bustle of luggage being packed in preparation for the journey to Vöslau. But that year, in Olmütz, there was nothing except fear to alter our routine. Nothing made me happy there anymore. Everything was increasingly bothersome; I felt rootless, and, at Aunt Alicia's house, fear, misgivings, weariness and intolerance had replaced the joy, excitement and expectation of the days prior to the *Purim* dance and the quiet contentedness of the following days, when we had found pleasure in our talks and our afternoon walks.

In the midst of that whirlwind of feelings, desires and frustrations, doubt and suspicion, predictions and realities, I kept asking myself the same question every night during that period of semi-consciousness that precedes deep sleep – in that state of tossing and turning where the unconscious mind, freed from the tensions of wakefulness, moves freely across a relaxed consciousness. The question that I asked myself over and over, ever since the day my father's phone call had changed my destiny, was: How can we have been so happy and not been aware of so much happiness? And while that question without an answer still hung in the air, I would fall into what should have been a refreshing sleep, but from which I always awoke a short time later with tears on my pillow, ready for a disturbing guest called insomnia to pay me its fearsome nightly visit.

MY PARENTS' ARRIVAL

Four months after the invasion of Austria, around July 15, we received a phone call from my father. It was the first time I had heard his voice since March, and I couldn't believe it. He and my mother were in Czechoslovakia – they had just crossed the border after fleeing Austria. Again, he was sparing with his words, but kept saying that he and my mother were all right and, above all, they were together. He asked me to stay calm and that we should be on the lookout for them, as they had no money and we would have to pay the cost of their taxi ride from the Czech border to Olmütz. "We'll tell you everything later," he said, ending the conversation.

They arrived around four hours later. It was a crushingly hot day and dehydration made them weaker than they already were. They seemed truly spent. However, despite the heat, they were both shaking as though they were cold, but the trembling was due to lack of food and sheer exhaustion. We hugged for a long time, crying and practically whimpering, saying words that were cut short by sobs, kissing one another again and again, until we all finally started laughing. We couldn't believe we were together again. Aunt Alicia and my mother immediately wanted to tell each other everything that had happened, but my father recommended prudence and said we should go upstairs to my aunt's rooms for protection. They had brought very little luggage with them and were dressed like Austrian mountain peasants, wearing typical Tyrolese outfits that they had never before worn in their lives. They were so weak that once upstairs, they asked for permission to lie down on a bed and they stretched out in their clothes. Then they began to tell us the story of their odyssey since the invasion of Austria. In the four months since then, they had overcome such

Ilse with her father.

a succession of aggressions, fear and risky situations that they felt as though a much longer time had elapsed.

My father, with his clear, organized mind, began the story at the beginning, describing what the Nazi invasion had been like and how life for them in Vienna had changed from one day to the next because of the immediate persecution of the Jews. He pointed out that it was not his intention to scare us, but simply to inform us objectively of what was going on, so that we might draw our own conclusions, learn from their experience and from now on be very careful about everything we did. He hinted that all of our possessions might already be in Nazi hands – which they were indeed – but he was generous enough not to say it in so many words, giving us room for hope.

Nazi antisemitism had spread across Vienna with devastating virulence. My father's tale confirmed what Aunt Alicia and I had heard on the BBC about Jews being the victims of all types of public offenses – they were spat upon, shoved around when they walked on the street, not allowed to use the sidewalks or the elevators of apartment buildings and were forced to sweep the streets. Their personal documents had also been taken from them, which meant that Jewish employees lost their jobs and business owners had their licenses revoked and their shops shut down, so that they and their families became increasingly vulnerable and destitute.

Seeking to escape from Austria, my parents had managed to get in touch with people who promised to get them the necessary papers to cross the border in exchange for money. My parents had paid the sum and accepted all the conditions, putting themselves in these people's hands. When the fixed day arrived, a car driven by an unknown man had picked them up and driven them towards Znaim, an outpost on the border with Czechoslovakia. My father seemed very upset when he told us this part of the story, and my mother cried intermittently. I dug my nails into the palms of my hands while listening in astonishment. Aunt Alicia and I had both heard that such things were going on, but to be certain of it and to have had it happen to my parents, magnified the imagined horror to the point that it was nearly tangible.

When the car had been 200 meters from the Znaim outpost – from where they had been promised they could cross from Austria into Czechoslovakia – four men in Gestapo uniforms (*Geheime Staatspolizei*, Secret State Police) showed up on two Nazi army motorcycles with sidecars and arrested my parents. Their driver, who was no doubt part of the gang that had betrayed them and taken their money, was allowed to go free, but my parents were jailed in two dingy little rooms, not much more than sheds, where my father had been watched over by a private and my mother by a woman who looked more like a peasant than a militiawoman. This deficient training on the part of the jailers, combined with my mother's relentless screams and protests as well as her crying and fainting episodes, which kept growing in intensity, resulted in her being freed while my father remained in jail. Undoubtedly, that border outpost had not come under military organization yet, and fortunately for my parents the whole incident had been either just a clumsy reflection of the invaders' real capacity for violence or else an act cooked up by the gang of traitors.

My mother had been able to return to Vienna by train after someone had given her a few coins for the fare. Back home, my mother had sought assistance from a lawyer friend with help from Berta, who had been left in charge of the house. The lawyer's intervention was wise, and after 15 to 20 days of paperwork, several meetings and very likely a cash payment, my father was free to go home. But the feeling of betrayal, the bitter taste of lost freedom and the confirmation that their personal situation was very fragile indeed in the midst of Austria's rampant antisemitism – especially in Vienna – had made my father seek a new means of escape.

Not surprisingly, my parents' circle of friends included individuals who offered them information about underground groups that took people out of the country in exchange for large sums of money, and whose members had contacts on the other side of the border to assist, protect and guide their clients during the first few moments of freedom. My father explained how cautiously and fearfully he had interviewed the people recommended by his friends. After the Znaim experience, everything sounded suspicious to him and he did not trust promises anymore. But, finally, he found some people who seemed trustworthy and, feeling the pressure from the daily acts of antisemitism in Vienna, he made a deal with the group and planned the escape.

On the agreed-upon day and time, my parents had left in their peasant clothes and driven in a rural vehicle to the place where they were to cross from Austria into Czechoslovakia. Protected by the shadows, they had dragged themselves under the barbed wire and over the thorny plants and rocky terrain. It had been an enormous effort and they had got numerous cuts and scratches on their hands and faces for their pains. Although they had been allowed to take one suitcase each, these remained inside the vehicle until the group was able to get them across into Czechoslovakia and deliver them – if my parents made it to the other side, that is. If not, the luggage would have disappeared. No doubt these people had special agreements with border police and army officials who facilitated these kinds of maneuvers.

When they finally found themselves on Czechoslovakian territory in the middle of the night, they had walked in spurts over uneven terrain and grazing fields, tripping and falling until it finally got light. With the danger now behind them, they sought out a path, then found a road, and later a town where some people who worked for the organization they had hired were waiting for them. These people returned their luggage, gave them some food and water, and my parents then phoned us and took a car with Czech license plates all the way to Olmütz.

We suggested that my father stop the tale there, as they both needed to eat and get some rest. We gave them everything they needed for a hot bath and made food and drinks to help them recover from so many exhausting hours of fasting and dehydration. I lovingly prepared one of the many rooms at Aunt Alicia's house so they could rest, and for the first time after several long days and hours fraught with anxiety, fear and suffering, they slept soundly.

Needless to say, my parents' long-awaited arrival introduced radical changes at Aunt Alicia's house, where we had finally settled into a routine that afforded us some stability, even if it did not bring me any personal joy. It had taken us a long time to organize our new life after my father's call telling me to remain in Olmütz, and even though the arrangement was not as beneficial to me as it was to my aunt, by now it had become so routine that we were used to it, or perhaps the correct term would be *resigned* to it. When my parents arrived, our immediate future changed once more. I again experienced that wonderful sense of protection that had always seemed to be there for me in Vienna, and it made me feel like I was recovering my freedom and could once again be the carefree young woman who had been shelved away for the last four months. For Aunt Alicia, however, these new guests – imposed on her by circumstances – signified a loss of privacy, and her annoyance, which became obvious almost immediately, quickly grew into an attitude of overt displeasure that made daily life difficult for everyone.

For the first few days, when the overall mood was still peaceful, my parents recovered from their efforts by eating right and sleeping long hours. In front of Aunt Alicia's house there was a very beautiful park with lush vegetation that had been in bloom since the spring, scenting the evening air. The water running down the park's many slopes filled the area with the fresh, musical sound of fountains. My parents spent a lot of time in that park, resting and trying to regain their composure. Occasionally, they chatted with my aunt's neighbors about the events taking place in Austria and the increasingly distressing news coming from there. I spent as much time with them as I could, but I had to keep seeing to my responsibilities as household manager, especially now that my parents were there and Aunt Alicia was unhappy about their presence. This situation was clearly more unpleasant for my father than for my mother, who considered it natural and acceptable to be a guest at her sister's, especially since Aunt Alicia, who loved the charms of Vienna, had been our own guest for prolonged periods of time on many occasions.

My father recovered in just a few days and seemed to have got in touch with himself again. He had regained that self-assurance that always defined him, and he immediately began planning how to get us out of this situation of dependence that we had unwillingly gotten ourselves into, and which grew more intolerable by the day. When you are accustomed to living in complete freedom, making the decisions that seem most convenient to you without consulting with anyone; when you are used to disposing of your own time and money, then it is truly difficult to deal with a situation such as ours. Lack of money was our main problem and that was due to the fact that the money in Jewish bank accounts had been confiscated when Austria was invaded. Since he was a banker, my father had learned about the Nazis' plans ahead of time and had managed to withdraw some of his own money, which he had taken home and kept in a hiding place. That money allowed them to cover their expenses in Vienna those first few months, although they were careful not to show that they were better off than other Jews. Later, they had spent a significant portion of that money on their first escape attempt, and the rest on their successful second attempt to leave Austria. By the time they reached Olmütz, they were penniless. As an emergency solution, my mother made a deal with Aunt Alicia that the latter would advance them money in exchange for a clasp that I had brought to Olmütz to wear at the *Purim* dance and which belonged to my mother.

The clasp was one of a three-piece set in which each piece was studded with diamonds, while the centerpiece in each case was a ruby, an emerald and a sapphire. The set had belonged to my Grandmother Mathilde Goldschmidt, who had given one piece to each of her two daughters and had kept the third for herself. All three parts could be joined together to form one single jewel, or else be used separately since they were esthetically complete. One belonged to my grandmother, one to my mother, and the third to Aunt Alicia. Later, in a bid to find a more substantial solution to our money problems, my father contacted a first cousin of his named Franz Joseph Hahn, who lived in Teplitz Schönau, the town where my father was born and where his entire family hailed from. Franz Joseph responded generously to the plea for help, and a few days later he sent us money so we could move to Prague. He said he would wait for us there and would help my father find a hotel and then an apartment where we might settle in more permanently.

By September, everything was ready for our move to Prague, and by *Rosh Hashanah* my parents and I were staying at the Alcron Hotel. With our life nearly back to normal, my father began contacting old acquaintances in international banking circles. Quickly, despite the limitations imposed on him by circumstances, he picked up the thread of his financial activities and began making money again. Everything seemed to indicate that we were headed for a comfortable life. A short time later, we were able to rent an apartment on Haštalská Str. 5, in the Altstadt (the Old City), and even hired a maid. For a while, we also managed to have a social life that was not as intense as the one we had had in Vienna, but which compensated me for the efforts and suffering at Aunt Alicia's house. Unfortunately, Franz Joseph Hahn, my father's first cousin whose help made it possible for us to enjoy this interval of comfort and well-being, died at the age of 28 inside a gas chamber in Auschwitz. His name appears on a memorial plaque at the Pinkas Synagogue[9] in Prague that pays tribute to the many Czechoslovakian Jews who were the victims of inhuman Nazi madness. When I first read his name there, I felt a great inner turmoil and deep pain.

The years we spent in Prague were a very important period in our lives, and my experiences there created an indelible memory in my mind. When I think back on Prague I get a feeling that I have trouble explaining rationally

9 The interior of the Pinkas synagogue, which was designed and executed by the painters Václav Boštík and Jiří John between 1954 and 1959, comprises 77,297 names of Czechoslovakian Jews who perished.

even today, despite the fact that, at this time of stocktaking, my mind has performed a retrospective analysis and assigned each event its true value, grouping the most relevant moments together in clear and objective synthesis. It is a strange feeling, a mix of joy and excitement, very typical of young girls, yet also tinged with fear and horror. They are memories that bring back feelings of hunger, deprivation and insecurity in a confusing whirlwind of images of war, sordid prisons, cruel murders and unimaginable atrocities. Despite all that, I retain the memory of Prague's great beauty, of its placid river and beautiful bridges, and these good memories include the birth of my son and the first time I felt his warm, trembling little body when a pair of kindly hands placed him on my pillow, in the hollow of my shoulder, brushing against my cheek. I will talk more about this later, when this story takes us there.

THE NAZI THREAT

There were several Viennese families who had fled Austria and taken refuge in Prague, including a few of my father's friends and many of my girlfriends. I remember that first period in the beautiful Czech capital as a happy, hopeful time. I was seeing friends from Vienna who expanded my social circle by introducing me not just to other Viennese youngsters, but to Czechoslovakian ones as well. Generally speaking, they were all Jewish and we had to stay alert and avoid potential denunciations. We got together at each other's homes, listened to music, danced, drank coffee and had spontaneous fun, the way youngsters always do. Other times, we went out for walks and that is how I became acquainted with many beautiful spots in Prague. Unfortunately, it all lasted a very short time. We were under threat from the Nazis and I felt scared again – I'm sure I was not the only one – but I didn't show it, perhaps out of a desire, even a need, to prolong that sense of well-being that I so desperately needed.

The second half of March 1939 had barely begun when German troops, who had already taken possession of the Sudetenland – an area inhabited by a German-speaking minority that was practically handed over to the Reich due to the weakness of Chamberlain and Daladier – occupied Czechoslovakia, creating the Protectorate of Bohemia and Moravia on the Führer's orders. Emil Hácha, the president of Czechoslovakia since November 30, 1938, was summoned by Hitler to the Reich Chancellery in Berlin. On March 15, 1939, Hácha was forced to sign a treaty putting the fate of the Czech people into the Führer's hands, while he retained his office as president of the new Protectorate.

Once again, the ghost of Nazism was besetting us. We started running into serious difficulties and found ourselves living in fear once again. We knew that bad things could happen at any moment. Meanwhile, Aunt Alicia had arrived in Prague one month earlier, in early February. Her car was the color of champagne except for the roof, which was brown, and her chauffeur wore a matching champagne-colored uniform with brown fasteners, in keeping with my aunt's aesthetic tastes. Aunt Alicia always paid attention to every last detail of her refined and elegant world, instead of considering that right now she was risking her own safety, as well as ours, at a time that called for extreme circumspection. A considerable number of suitcases and boxes containing her jewels and silver were unloaded from the car and deposited in our apartment. She was fleeing Olmütz, on Moravian territory, for Prague, which – rumor had it – would not be occupied. Now she was the one who needed protection, and needless to say, she got it.

Following advice from her boyfriend Otto Sametz, who was the director of the Union Bank, she leased two safe-deposit boxes at that institution, the biggest bank in Prague. In the larger box – which was very large indeed – she placed her fine silverware, which altogether weighed approximately 50 kilograms; and in the smaller one she left most of her jewels, taking the rest to our house. It was considered prudent back then to protect one's luxury goods ahead of potential house searches, but at the same time it was convenient to have a few items handy, in case it became necessary to use them as payment for safe conduct out of the Nazi danger zone, or simply to buy food. My parents' own experience, as well as similar situations encountered by a few Jewish friends in Austria, underscored the need for this kind of precautionary measure.

The danger was growing greater by the day, and later it started increasing by the hour. Finally, on March 15, 1939, the German Army entered Prague. I think it is almost unnecessary to describe how we felt that day. What we were all afraid of was now a reality, and it was camped outside our door. Without asking for permission or even announcing their intentions, the Nazis began entering as many households as they pleased – those they suspected of containing Jewish families, or families who opposed their heartless regime. The city they invaded showed its rejection by greeting them with empty streets, and the sidewalk echoed with the arrogant sound of their boots, their caterpillar tanks, their dogs' barks and their rough voices yelling out harsh orders.

Even though it was a risky thing to do, I wanted to go down to the street and see the invasion with my own eyes. I knew that when Vienna was invaded, a vast majority of the Viennese population had welcomed the German Army with cries of joy. It is hard to believe, but that is the way it was. In Prague, however, the predominant attitude of the Czechoslovakian people was one of absolute contempt. I saw it as I stood there, my back pressed firmly against a wall that I wished I could blend into to remain unnoticed on that solitary street where only German troops were to be seen. I felt it on my skin and all the way down to my bone marrow when I heard the boots echoing in the surrounding silence. I was witness to the cold reception that the residents of Prague expressed so eloquently by locking themselves up at home, shutting their windows, pulling down their blinds and turning out their lights. Later, I would see worse things – heartbreaking and atrocious things – but the memory of that invasion is still fresh in my mind.

The Nazis did not stick around long. On Saturday, March 18, in mid-afternoon, the door of our apartment yielded to repeated hammering and blows by eight Gestapo men. They came in with their guns cocked and forced us to face the wall with our hands in the air, treating us with no consideration at all, shoving us and yelling at us the entire time. It was the empire of fear extending its territorial right into our home, where we knew the Nazis would show no mercy and shoot us at the slightest suspicious movement. They were looking for money, jewels or documents that might compromise us. But they did not find a thing, and that made them angrier than ever. They left, promising to return. We had hidden Aunt Alicia's jewels, some money my father had earned, and a few important documents inside sugar, rice and noodle tins, and also among the firewood, by the fireplace. It did not occur to them to look amongst the kitchen things or the firewood, although they would not have failed to do so given a little more experience or training. We were terrified. The moment they had gone, and after making sure that nobody had stayed behind to listen at the door or on the staircase, we tried to calm down and my father said we had to leave the apartment immediately and move to a safer place. We were, in fact, going into hiding, which was a terrible measure since we had done nothing wrong, committed no crime to justify such a move. But reality demanded it: Our lives were in danger.

I remembered that the family of a student at the Art Academy in Vienna, where I had studied performing arts while he studied to be a pianist, was living in Prague. This young man, who was quite slovenly and did not have very good manners, had once asked my father for my hand in marriage at the age of 16, even though I had not wanted him as my fiancé. This had upset my father, who sent him away with his tail between his legs. When I brought up his family name as a possible solution to our troubles in Prague, I failed to remember this unfortunate incident, nor did my father make the connection. After speaking to the family and settling on the conditions, my parents moved to the young man's house to hide there. Meanwhile, Aunt Alicia committed herself to Dr. Gottlieb's clinic in Weinbergen in the hope of finding protection by posing as a patient. Dr. Gottlieb was a Jewish doctor and a friend of hers. I decided to stay at the apartment so I could pack our most necessary items and look for a new place to live.

However, it turned out that my former schoolmate's family began extracting money from my parents in return for protection, so my father decided that the best way to escape antisemitic persecution, which was already full blown, would be for all of us to join Aunt Alicia at Dr. Gottlieb's clinic. On March 20, once the conditions had been agreed upon, my father and mother were admitted as patients, while I went along as their dependent. This curious shelter turned out to be safe but very expensive, and since our new situation made it impossible for my father to work, we had to watch our expenses. I returned carefully and sporadically to our apartment, and from there searched for a guesthouse or hotel to which we might all move. But on Tuesday, March 28, several Gestapo men walked into the Gottlieb Clinic and took my father away. My mother, thinking he was being taken to a concentration camp, went into a panic and tried to commit suicide. It was a very tense and distressing situation because we were unable to calm her down, and the clinic workers refused to assist her until they were sure that the Nazis had left the establishment entirely. Danger ruled and people looked out for themselves. Any attitude deemed confusing to German eyes, or any movement they considered suspicious, could result in a wave of machine-gun fire, ending the life of the person in question as well as everyone else in the vicinity.

DESPERATE TO ESCAPE FROM HELL

Aunt Alicia, who still had her Czechoslovakian passport, had applied for a visa to travel to Paris to get out of a hellish situation that was already starting to go up in flames. Since she was very weak, I went to the French Embassy with her to help with the paperwork, and later to the Gestapo offices where more forms had to be filled out before she could leave the country.

In German-occupied Czechoslovakia, visa applicants who were Jewish had to declare their belongings at one of the offices that the Gestapo ran in various parts of the country for the control, inventory and appraisal of these goods. The declared items were carefully listed and described, and the owner received a copy of the list of appraised goods. Nothing was taken away and the owners kept their valuables, but this way the government knew what each Jew owned and what it was worth. On Monday, April 3, I accompanied Aunt Alicia to help her with this dubious procedure, as she was very scared. We had to take her gems to a jewelry shop that was authorized by the Gestapo to carry out appraisals, and two of their delegates took an entire day to record and appraise the many jewels that Aunt Alicia declared in hopes of obtaining her visa to France. I was just 18, but dealing with all these situations that were so alien to made me feel like I was ageing at a much faster pace than normal. I was getting used to tackling problems no matter what their size, and whenever I felt scared I somehow always managed to overcome my fear without really knowing how I did it or how long my courage would last. In my emotional fencing match with terror, I guess I was just not ready to yield, and even though I often had an ice-cold feeling in my veins, I somehow knew that the privilege of the final thrust lay in my own hands.

Everything was going according to plan. On Saturday, April 8, 1939, Aunt Alicia left Prague for Paris. She had finally obtained her visa, and although she had had to turn in all her jewels, her silverware still sat undeclared in the safe-deposit box at the Union Bank. My mother and I were left all alone in Prague. We had no news of my father. The Gottlieb Clinic, where we were still living, had become prohibitively expensive. We had very little money left, since neither my mother nor I had access to the safe that my father had leased at the Alcron Hotel in order to conceal a sum of money wired to him from abroad. Besides, the clinic no longer felt safe, because if the Nazis had come to take my father away, there was no reason they could not return for us as well. I therefore decided this problem had to be solved immediately and my mother and I agreed that we had to move.

Before moving to the clinic, I had already looked around for a place to stay and one of the possibilities had been the beautiful and traditional Hotel Flora, located on Orlicka Street in Prague. We moved there on April 10 or 11. Once we were settled in, and feeling safer already, I thought about obtaining visas for my parents and myself to get out of Czechoslovakia, which was becoming increasingly dangerous. I already knew how the application system worked at the French Embassy, so I went back hoping for success, since my Austrian passport was still in order. Even though my parents had been stripped of theirs, I knew there were underground organizations in Prague that could provide people with "extra-official" papers for the right sum of money.

However, an unexpected surprise was awaiting me at the French Embassy. While waiting my turn, a young man of around 20, whom I hadn't noticed until then, walked up to me. When I heard his voice, I looked up and there – without his military uniform but looking more handsome than I remembered him – stood my Prince Charming, the one who had waltzed with me in Olmütz at that unforgettable *Purim* dance. Willy Groak – that was his name – was holding out his hand to me and smiling and his laughing eyes seemed glued to mine. Our pupils moved with the excited movements and blissful gleam of a lover's gaze when the beloved one is finally found. It was a magical moment during which old memories resurfaced, making me relive the sensuality of that waltz and the touch of his strong arm around my waist. Before I had fully recovered from the excitement of our reunion, he adopted a mysterious air and asked if I had enjoyed receiving a bunch of violets each day, happily confirming my suspicions regarding that matter. Those violets had been very significant to me since they had filled the days following the dance with excitement, and later with hope, after my father's life-changing phone call forced me to stay in Olmütz in such unfavorable conditions. Those violets had been my loyal confidants as I quietly fell in love with their sender, and were my faithful companions during those never-ending nights of exhausting insomnia. The last ones he had sent me were still lying between the pages of *Faust*, my favorite book.

My life was in upheaval once again, but this time it felt wonderful. From that moment, Willy and I carried on an unforgettable romance and a sweet, innocent engagement, which is how young lovers did things back then. I do not want to be the judge of whether that type of relationship was better or worse than the ones that are fashionable and admissible these days; I am simply explaining how engagements worked then. But I do want to say that even if we were never as intimate as young lovers are today, we were immensely happy and the limits imposed on us by the rules of our time never put a damper on the joys of love. From that day on we shared the enormous emotional baggage that comes from experiencing the distress of a pre-war period – enhanced by the fact that we were both Jewish. We kept each other company as much as we could, considering he had to continue with his engineering studies and I had to keep helping my parents. We weaved dreams together, enjoying the bliss of love but remaining aware of our responsibilities. We met nearly every day, going on long walks through lovely Prague, enjoying the spring and then the summer, with the Moldau[10] – an important feature of that beautiful landscape – providing solace from the summer heat. We tried to have fun, which was not easy in the current atmosphere. Willy's family was afraid because my father was constantly being hounded by the Gestapo. The Nazis knew he was an international banker with connections and money in other countries, and this was of great interest to them. Since Willy and I had fallen in love, however, we were afraid of nothing and nobody. The world was at our feet.

I had run into Willy a few days after Aunt Alicia's departure. Around a week later, possibly on April 15, she phoned the clinic asking to speak to us. She was informed that we no longer lived there, but since they knew her personally, they gave her our new telephone number. She called the Hotel Flora and asked us to pick her up at the Prague prison, where she had been taken after being arrested on her way out of Czechoslovakia, despite having her passport and visa in order and having turned in her belongings, as demanded of her. She was ill and weak. It was a tough blow to see her like that. I had been calm on her account, thinking she was free in Paris, but here she was once again in Prague, in a pitiful and worrisome state of exhaustion. For me, it was an added problem and one more cause for concern: I knew absolutely nothing about my father, and my mother and I were running out of money. We went to get Aunt Alicia from the jail and took her back to the hotel with us, but then

10 Vltava in Czech – the river that crosses and runs through Prague.

decided she should return to her house in Olmütz because we could not afford to pay accommodation for three people. So Aunt Alicia went home, sick and without her luggage, since both her trunks with her clothes and other belongings, including her toilet bag, had been left on the Paris-bound train when she was arrested and sent back to Prague.

NEWS ABOUT MY FATHER

A few days later, our inquiries about my father finally yielded some results and we learned that he had been held at a police station that had some kind of connection to the Gestapo. From there he had been transferred to Pankrác prison, a sordid and fearsome place, where my mother and I managed to visit him one night, after jumping over numerous bureaucratic hurdles. I never imagined I would see my father in such a state. He was physically gaunt and emotionally distraught, and I could see from the marks and dried blood caked on the purplish skin of his face, arms and hands that he had been beaten. He kept whimpering "hungry, hungry" over and over. I had brought him a sandwich, thinking he would enjoy the taste of homemade food, but I was not allowed near him and could not give it to him. I was 18 years old, and like I said at the beginning of this story, I dearly loved my father. The distress of seeing him in such a deplorable state was so tremendous that I broke down and started crying and screaming like a small child. I was fully aware that this reaction was the worst thing I could do for that person whom I loved so much, but it was precisely the great love I felt for him that was now betraying me. I felt exhausted after having had to deal with so many problems in the last few months, and knowing there was nothing I could do to help my father threw me into despair. All the while, my mother remained calm and a Czech guard who was in the room with us picked me up off the floor and hid me, saying that if I didn't shut up, the Germans would jail me and kill me. When my emotional crisis was over, we returned to the hotel. Once I had calmed down, I was able to think things over and concluded that even if my father was in a bad condition, at least he was still alive, and that was reason enough for hope.

Sixty days after his arrest at the Gottlieb Clinic, my father was released. But eight days later, around June 4, he was arrested again while walking down the street, because the Germans mistook him for Otto Hahn, a German physicist and chemist who, together with Fritz Strassmann[11] and Lise Meitner, first formulated a theory about the fission of heavy nuclei in 1938, a feat that would earn him a Nobel Prize in Chemistry in 1944. It was precisely the fields of physics and chemistry that Dr. Hahn specialized in that worried the Reich so much, because they led directly to the creation of new weapons which, years down the line, would include the atomic bomb. When my father's real identity was confirmed, the Gestapo allowed him to go free.

Our lives seemed peaceful once again. We were staying at the Hotel Flora, where we each had a room, although these rooms were not adjacent and were in fact quite far from each other. But we lived comfortably, and having my father nearby made me feel safe again. We were still struggling financially, a common problem for most Jews at the time, since they had been stripped of their belongings or else could not access them because they had hidden them away. Such was my father's case with the money that was wired to him from abroad and which he kept in a secret safe-deposit box at the Hotel Alcron, where Nazi surveillance made it difficult to walk in unnoticed. Sometime later, the Gestapo would confiscate the box, making our situation even more difficult than it already was.

Willy Groak and I were still in love and we went as far as to exchange engagement rings. I was 18 and he was 23. He was my first love and I was walking on air. Willy was planning to travel to what was then Palestine, where preparations were firmly underway for the creation of the State of Israel, which would see the light nine years later, providing us Jews with the country that we had always needed. When I found out that he might be leaving, I went mad and cried so much and for so many days that he finally dropped his plans. This was the first shadow cast over our romance.

It was early July and it was hot. One morning before breakfast, I went to my father's room as usual to wish him a good morning, but I found the door ajar and thought that he must have gotten up earlier than usual. I knocked softly and got no response. I knocked again, harder this time. All I got was silence. I pushed the door open and a shiver ran down my spine: My father was not there.

11 Fritz Strassmann was recognized by Yad Vashem as a Righteous Among the Nations on July 16, 1985. In March 1943, he concealed Andrea Wolffenstein, a Jewish woman sought by the Gestapo, at his home until she found an alternative place outside Berlin. He died in Mainz in 1980.

His bed was unmade and the whole room was a mess. I looked for the maid and when she saw me she started to cry. Early in the morning, she sobbed, some Gestapo men had stormed in and taken him away, naturally without saying to where.

Once again, we fell prey to fear and distress. Again we felt the anguish of not knowing where my father was. We were aware that this kind of thing was happening all the time and that many Jews were being unexpectedly arrested without being told why. But each time my father disappeared we slipped into a depression that was at first all-consuming and then reverted into a state of boundless agitation as we started to snap out of it. There was little we could do, because the mystery surrounding these arrests forced us to act with great shrewdness and discretion, suppressing all outward signs of distress, tears or indignation in a heartless, destructive game that gradually sapped our strength.

In that atmosphere of authoritarianism that had pervaded Prague since the Nazi invasion, antisemitism was clearly on the rise in all aspects of daily existence and all walks of life. One had to be very careful not to make any wrong moves. We even had to feign indifference to events that moved us to the marrow of our bones, as did all the people whose loved ones were brutally taken away from them. It was necessary to behave with supreme coolness while a fire of pain burned our insides; it was essential to speak serenely even when what one really wanted to do was scream like a wounded animal; and we had to learn to look at things with dry eyes even when a river of tears, contained by our eyelids, threatened to brim over and unleash a flow of bitterness. That pleasant sense of harmony we thought we had attained when all three of us were living together at the Hotel Flora was suddenly gone. Again our lives were in turmoil. Everything around us was turning into a problem. The news was more alarming by the day – Germany was not satisfied with the occupation of Austria and Czechoslovakia; it wanted the entire world. War was imminent and the Germans knew how they would trigger it. Suddenly, in Prague, there was complete lack of freedom. The streets became virtually empty and if two people were seen talking together, a soldier patrol would interrogate them separately regarding the topic of their conversation. If the answers did not coincide, both people were either arrested or shot on the spot. The news from Olmütz was no better. People there were living in fear as well.

THE LOSS OF A FIRST LOVE

Willy Groak's family started opposing our engagement. My father's latest arrest was causing unrestrained panic among Willy's relatives, which was having a negative effect on our relationship and, soon after, led to its end. By mid-August 1939, Willy and I had stopped seeing each other.

There is no question that when harmony is broken the consequences of the fracture cause a chain reaction that progressively destroys every single one of the elements it had used to bond together. Only great fortitude and a clear, cold mind that is able to come up with the right strategy can pull someone out of such a situation. I sensed as much, but where was my strength? How could I possibly think, plan and act with a clear, cold mind if my mind was awhirl with the anxiety of broken dreams and lost love, especially when I most needed my beloved's support, and all because my father had been arrested by the Nazis and everyone else was scared? And who were they anyway to interfere with my life? During that sorrowful time I learned how bitter and complicated losing your first love can be. Much later, I would also learn that one's first love is usually unforgettable.

Once again, insomnia was my guest on those long summer nights, just as it had been the previous summer in Olmütz. Once again, great big splotches of tears drew the map of my grief on the pillow. Once again, I knew I had to go out there and fight against adversity, because no amount of nighttime crying would deliver me from suffering or retrieve lost happiness, nor would it solve the problems I had and would continue to have for a long time to come. I also knew that this chronic crying would not, suddenly and magically, bring my father back to me safe and sound.

I was now faced with the repeatedly difficult task of finding out where my father was being held. Once more I was in despair thinking that he might have been killed or ill-treated and tortured as he had been at the Pankrác prison. Yet again my questions would be left without answers, the doors I knocked on would remain shut, and the telephones would keep ringing without anybody bothering to pick up. Confusion, impotence and indignation threatened to take hold of me once more. But, above all, I felt alone. I *was* alone – absolutely and completely. But I was ready to fight.

THE BBC WORLD SERVICE

The political and military situation was more and more alarming. Newscasts were under Nazi control and genuine information could only be obtained by listening to the BBC, which was not only difficult at the time, but also dangerous as it was forbidden by the Gestapo. The manager of the Hotel Flora, where my mother and I were staying, had been born in Košice and he had that special gift for languages that is so typical of certain Central Europeans. He spoke French, English, Italian and Slovenian in addition to German, Czech (he had lived in Prague most of his life) and Hungarian, his mother tongue.

This man had a radio that could pick up the BBC's broadcasts from London and he used to invite a group of around 15 Jewish hotel guests up to his room on the top floor, where they followed the distressing reports about the advance of the German Army and the Reich's policies, which were clearly leading to World War II. The BBC also provided information about the antisemitic activities that the Nazis were engaged in, especially in the occupied countries. The manager invited me to these get-togethers and I gladly accepted. I wanted to know the truth about what was going on, and it also made me feel better to be surrounded by other Jews, because I knew I could trust them. Perhaps, even subconsciously, I hoped that one of them might know something about my father or provide a lead as to where to find him. Those meetings also allowed me to be with people at a time when loneliness weighed so heavily on me.

The room next to the manager's was occupied by the deputy manager, a man whose last name was Kitler and who was a known Nazi sympathizer. Kitler was mistrustful of this group of people who met with his colleague so quietly and mysteriously every day. The two rooms shared a balcony, which made meeting there all the more dangerous at a time when the Gestapo had tightened regulations against Jews.

WAR, A TERRIER AND TRUE FRIENDSHIP

Finally, on September 1, 1939, Poland was invaded. The Germans had achieved what they so badly wanted: the outbreak of World War II. There was panic – a secret, quiet panic – among Jewish families. We all asked ourselves what would become of us, what would become of the entire world, how long this madness would last. We were barely at the beginning of the war and before reaching the end we would endure six painful years of cruelty and extermination. That same night a curfew was imposed and we were forbidden from going out after a certain time. Sirens went off and it was mandatory to shut our windows and turn off the lights. Beautiful Prague was beginning to dress as if in mourning.

November came round and it started getting cold. As autumn progressed, night extended its shadowy presence and the days started getting shorter. Prague turned ocher like the leaves on its trees, and the frequent rains left a layer of dampness on its walls and sidewalks, making everything look very sad. We still had no news of my father. We were careful about how much money we spent, but everything kept getting more expensive and our lives were becoming more limited due to our lack of resources. The meetings in the manager's room had been suspended, because the Gestapo was watching to ensure that the ban on radio newscasts from countries opposed to Nazism was observed. A growing feeling of depression began sapping our spirits.

Inside the hotel and in the midst of this pervading sadness, there was a cute little terrier that livened up everyone's day. Its name was Toy and its owner was Carlos Brunel, the diplomatic representative of the Argentine Republic in Czechoslovakia, who was staying at the Hotel Flora with his wife Celia and their daughter Coqui. Brunel spoke perfect French, therefore when Toy had to be seen by a vet, the hotel manager went along to translate the vet's indications from Czech into French. This helped strengthen the friendship that had already emerged between these men through their common love of French literature and art.

The day that the manager decided to put an end to the meetings, he told me that if I was interested, I could keep going up to his room to listen to the radio because in the event of a room search, he would say I was his girlfriend and that was the reason I was there with him. By then we had become friends and trusted each other. He was a very cultivated man, quite shy, extremely respectful and 13 years my elder – he was 32 and I had just turned 19. For this reason he treated me as if he were my father, though with great formality. He could sense my sadness and knew that the reason was not just my father's disappearance, but also the breakup with Willy, whom he had always seen in my company.

Carlos Brunel, the Argentine consul in Prague during World War II, with his wife and daughter.

SERIOUS MONEY CONCERNS

It was not long before our money situation started to become alarming. I informed the manager of the Hotel Flora that we would be moving, as we could no longer afford to pay for our rooms. His reaction was to offer me part of his own meager savings to help us stay at the hotel, which was safe and decent. I thanked him but told him I would look for less expensive accommodation that we could afford on our scant resources. He said he thought it would be very difficult to conduct such a search in our present circumstances – an observation that was not exactly news to me. I was still a teenager, almost penniless, Jewish, without protection, and lost in the middle of a pack of anti-semitic wolves who were occupying Prague. It was the ideal recipe for failure and I knew it. I suddenly had that horrible feeling that had been lurking inside me for some time, waiting to resurface again: fear.

Nevertheless, faced with imminent poverty that threatened to deprive us of food and shelter, I remembered I still had one weapon left: my deceased

Uncle Marko Heller's legacy. In order to have the right to that money, it was necessary for me to get married, as Aunt Alicia's husband had clearly indicated in his notarized will that it was a wedding gift for me and his two other nieces, Liese and Gerty Friedmann, the daughters of his sister Josefine. It was suddenly imperative that I get married, but would this alleged solution not be even harder to achieve than an inexpensive room for my mother and me? And even if I managed to marry just for the sake of the inheritance, would that not be tantamount to betraying my Uncle Marko's generous and romantic intentions? And what about that other legacy, the one I received from my elders, which consisted of respect for the family and for the institution of marriage? My only answer to this and to all the other questions was another question: Was it disrespectful to the institution of marriage to plan my wedding for such an apparently materialistic reason? But then I would encourage myself with more upbeat thoughts, telling myself with great conviction that I could make a happy home out of a marriage begun in such peculiar circumstances. After all, had I not faced very difficult challenges in the last few months and always found a solution to each and every problem?

While I tormented myself with this whirlwind of questions and concerns, something told me that what was ultimately on the line was life itself, our lives, and as a Jewish person I had been raised to respect God in the first place and then life above everything else. Do we not drink to something with the toast "*L'Chayim*," which means "To life" or "For life"? And so, alternately being harsh on myself and justifying my intentions, I slowly quelled the anxiety produced by this daily game of light and darkness whose final score I always unconsciously ensured would be favorable to my plans.

So once again I was forced to make a vitally important decision and take full responsibility for my actions: I would marry the manager of the Hotel Flora. Although my decision was based on the need to access the money that my Uncle Marko Heller had left me in his will, it was not a completely random choice. Over the course of several months, as our meetings to listen to the BBC newscasts gave way to a solid friendship, I had the chance to observe many positive aspects to his personality: He was a decent man, respectful, formal and protective. On the other hand, his negative points were mainly his marked shyness and a tendency to seek out solitude and silence. But he was intelligent, loved books and music — he was an excellent pianist — and was always keen to learn. He was the son of a countryside doctor and his habits were simple, as provincial folks' habits usually are. He had paid his way through engineering school by working as a tour guide in Italy during the summer months and other student holidays, and this had not only allowed him to earn some money, but also to perfect his Italian.

This man, who had always treated me protectively, almost paternally, and who always showed nothing but respect and affection for me, was so shocked when I proposed to him that the only thing he managed to articulate was that the whole thing was impossible. He argued that he had never so much as given a moment's thought to marriage; that in any case it should be his decision to make, not mine; that he was unprepared both mentally and emotionally to face such a responsibility; and that, in short, my proposal was beyond the limits of his own logic. But I was unfazed. I explained once again about my Uncle Marko Heller's will. I offered to marry him with the promise of splitting up once I obtained the money. I told him I really needed this money to save my mother's life, my own life, even my father's life, since I was sure he was either in jail or maybe in a concentration camp – never once admitting the possibility, either consciously or unconsciously, that he might be dead. His refusal got weaker after my reiterated explanations and insistence, but I did not get the "yes" that I was after. And despite his flat refusal, I guessed that his protective and paternal attitude towards me would remain unchanged.

Suddenly, a very alarming thing happened. The manager of the Hotel Flora was removed from his post on account of being Jewish. He was allowed to continue living there, in a smaller room, but he could no longer run the establishment. Was this a decision imposed by the Gestapo or a precautionary measure by hotel authorities? In either case, it was a new instance of antisemitism and in this case, it hit very close to home. There was a lot of restlessness at the hotel, since many of us were Jewish. Fear gripped us once again.

When he heard the news, Doctor Brunel immediately asked the manager if he could manage to learn Spanish within a month, so he could work as a secretary at the Argentine Consulate in Prague, which answered to the Argentine Embassy in Germany. The answer was swift: Yes, he could learn Spanish in a month. The ease with which he could learn languages, together with his intelligence and tenacity, enabled him to speak Spanish fluently within the month, and he was named Brunel's personal secretary. This appointment not only afforded him the security of regular wages – a very important thing after losing his job at the Hotel Flora – it also granted him some degree of diplomatic immunity, which was even more important for a Jewish person living in Prague in 1939.

When Ambassador Brunel spent time at the embassy headquarters in Hamburg, he was represented in Prague by the chargé d'affaires Thomas A. Manson, a man whose advancing blindness greatly limited his capacity for work. For this reason, Brunel began to delegate more responsibilities and increasingly important affairs to his secretary and friend, the former manager of the Hotel Flora. Meanwhile, I was still bent on getting married, so I decided to write a letter to the manager's father and send him a photograph of myself taken at the age of 15, which I always carried with me. My goal was to gain his support, so I explained who I was, how I had met his son and how we had become friends. I explained my situation and why I wanted to marry him: His moral integrity was a guarantee to me; only with such a man could I negotiate such a delicate matter.

A few days later the reply arrived by mail. His father fully endorsed my initiative, and wrote that my letter proved that I was an intelligent and decisive person, while my photograph showed I was young, all of which led him to believe that I would be able to persuade his son to marry me. He graciously added that if his son refused, it would be out of lack of intelligence on his part. All of this made my friend smile when he read his father's letter, but the "yes" I yearned for did not escape his lips, neither in Czech, German, French, nor in his recently learned Spanish.

I also wrote a letter to Aunt Alicia. I felt outwardly sure of my decision to marry for the money that her husband had left me, but I unconsciously sought out her opinion as a form of support, because I felt spiritually lonely — my father was absent, my mother did not have an opinion, and my future husband did not actually know that he would be marrying me, or indeed that he was my fiancé at all, even though we were just days away from the wedding. I was lucky enough to receive Aunt Alicia's reply by the next mail delivery. In her letter, she offered support and any help she could provide, given the difficult circumstances she was in herself — circumstances, which she explained in simple, anxiety-ridden sentences, were truly terrifying. She knew she could lose the right to live in her own home, which would certainly and immediately be occupied by a Nazi family. This was already happening to some Jewish families, so her fears were not groundless.

Although Aunt Alicia's letter was full of that same sweetness that I had felt from her in my childhood, and even though her support for my wedding plans was exactly what I needed and expected of her — that was the reason I had written to her in the first place — her other news filled me with grief and a bitter sense of defeat, something unknown to me until then, and these feelings upset me for several days. I could not accept the idea that all Jews were being deprived not just of their belongings, but, even more importantly, of the right to live in their own homes. I made a great effort to overcome this feeling; I could not allow myself to be dominated by all this madness, especially when nobody knew how much longer it might last. I had to carry out my plan, get married, claim the money Marko Heller had left me, and use it to escape from that hell-hole that threatened to devour us, humiliated and belittled by the arrogance of the people who fanned its diabolical flames.

With a firm purpose, I began filling out the marriage paperwork. My mind was made up. I went to the Old and New Synagogue in Prague, the synagogue that is so dear to all Jews and which was built around 1270, and I spoke with Rabbi Aladar Deutsch, explaining my situation: My father had disappeared, my mother was incapable of dealing with anything, we would have to leave the Hotel Flora because we were nearly penniless, and I had a chance — if I got married — of receiving an inheritance that was vitally important to us in our present situation.

The first observation that the rabbi made was that I was still underage, and that in order to get married I would need papers declaring me of legal age. So I went to the German Tribunal and saw a man named Doctor Raab, who showed that he was not a Nazi by agreeing to have me declared of legal age, thus allowing me to conduct my own business without permission from anyone. I returned triumphantly to the synagogue and the rabbi appointed two men he trusted — Izak Gerson and Simon Osterreicher — to accompany me on my bureaucratic errands. They were both elderly men, in fact they were close to 80, and there was at least one occasion when I was wittily asked if either one of them was the groom.

I obtained the papers declaring that I was of marriageable age and decided with the rabbi that the wedding would take place on May 25 at 11 in the morning, but then I immediately remembered that this was Argentina's national day and there would be an official event at the embassy, which my future husband would have to attend. "Not the twenty-fifth," I said firmly. "You had better make it the twenty-sixth, at ten in the morning." As usual when something frightened me, I felt a shiver run down my spine. The next step was still more difficult: Informing the manager of the Hotel Flora of the day and time of his own wedding and confirming that I would be his bride.

My decision seemed abnormal and whimsical and I knew it, but I also knew that we were living in the midst of such madness that nothing could really seem strange anymore. As far as the manager was concerned, I could see beyond his shy and prudent attitude, and was certain that he not only liked me but that he was in fact already in love with me. It had been a little over a month since I had unilaterally decided to marry the now former manager of the Hotel Flora, and with all the paperwork ready, I gathered up my courage and informed him that the wedding would take place in three days. "What wedding?" he asked in a puzzled tone. "Yours and mine," I answered with a firm voice that left no room for his personal opinion. With a gesture that revealed the confusion he felt at this piece of news, he hit his forehead with the palm of his right hand and exclaimed: "Oh, all right! But in that case, I want to buy you a wedding dress. What time is the ceremony?"

On our wedding day, my mother and I went to the synagogue together, but the manager – that is to say, my fiancé – showed up alone. I never saw a more cheerless wedding, with me wearing a black dress because of the sorrow I felt at the disappearance of my father, who could just as well have been dead for all we knew. In my hands, I carried a very small bunch of lilies that I had ordered the day before at a flower shop and my forehead and eyes were covered with a short veil made of white tulle, in accordance with synagogue rules. Happily, the small bunch of flowers made me feel better because of its fresh, spring-like scent that reminded me of our mornings at the Veilchen Villa. As we waited for the witnesses, who were none other than the two elderly men the rabbi had sent along with me on my errands two days earlier, I suddenly felt overwhelmed by a rush of images and feelings that forced me to pull myself together.

THERE WAS A CELEBRATION

The witnesses arrived and so did the manager – my fiancé – and we all entered the synagogue where the wedding was to be held. My mother did not utter a single word either before, during or after the ceremony. The rabbi's voice was a whisper in the empty temple and it only rang out at the culminating moment when he pronounced our names and asked if we consented to be joined in matrimony: "Edith Ilse Hahn, do you take Adalbert Kaufmann to be your husband?" To which I naturally replied: "I do." "Adalbert Kaufmann, do you take Edith Ilse Hahn to be your wife?" Fortunately, he also replied: "I do." When I say "fortunately," it is not simply because at the time I needed his "I do" so badly, but also because later in life Adalbert Kaufmann would prove to be a good husband, a good father and a good partner. He was basically — by nature and through his grandfather and mother's upbringing — a good person.

The rabbi completed the ritual and we left the ancient temple that was steeped in centuries' worth of history and tradition. It was a radiant spring morning. Light green leaves were budding on the trees and the cries of the swallows were so loud that it would have been hard to overhear our conversation, had there been any. We were all quite silent, although it is possible that we managed to express a few good wishes…at least that is all that I seem to remember about that day.

We went back to the hotel. Those who knew about the wedding congratulated us warmly and wished us the best of luck. The new hotel management had a wonderful lunch brought to our room and my brand-new husband, my silent mother and I ate it together. Later, the two of us took a walk through the parks of Vinohrady and other green areas of Prague that were already in bloom. I was happy at that moment and thought that soon our luck would improve and everything would work out the way we wanted. Youth is that period in life when almost everyone is optimistic no matter what their vital circumstances. I was young then and my youth was still very similar to my adolescence. In some ways, I was still almost a child.

MY HUSBAND'S FAMILY

Up until now I have referred to my husband as "the manager." But who was Adalbert (or Vojtech, in his native tongue) Kaufmann? Who was the man whose destiny was now joined to mine? What was his family like? And what happened to them?

Bela, as he was known, was born on July 22, 1907, in a small town near Košice, the capital of Eastern Slovakia, near the river Hornád. Bela was the son of Jindrich Kaufmann, a country doctor, and Regina Enkel. The couple

Vojtech (Adalbert) Kaufmann, Ilse's husband.

had three children: Erna, my husband Adalbert and Clara. Regina Enkel had already passed away by the time I met Bela.

The Kaufmanns were good people, as country folk tend to be. Erna, who as far as I can remember, was the eldest of the three children, married a lawyer named Nikulas Gavaller. Since surnames are defined by gender in the Czech language, upon marriage Erna became Mrs. Gavallerova. They had a little girl named Veruska Gavallerova. Clara, the youngest sibling, married Martin Erdely. All of them, except for Clara and my husband, perished at Auschwitz. But Veruska and her mother Erna had a particularly cruel and inhumane death. I would even call it a savage death. Clara, who was being detained at the same camp as her sister and young niece, later explained what happened – and it is a chilling tale.

Erna was pregnant with her second child when they were all deported to the concentration camp, and as usual, men and women were sent to different sections. Eventually, she gave birth to a baby boy who was immediately grabbed by a guard and hurled onto a bonfire along with little Veruska. In her despair, the mother threw herself against the guard to try to prevent such a crime, but a wave of machine-gun fire ended her life as well. It is difficult to talk about something so cruel, but why keep quiet about an event that so clearly defines the Nazi regime's policy? One need only look at the photograph of a happy Erna with her husband on their wedding day, and of little Veruska playing with her doll to appreciate the innocence of the newlyweds and their child, and gauge the degree of infamy that took their lives. How many more Veruskas were there, I wonder?

Much later, Clara left that inferno on what was known as the "death march." Nearly everyone perished along the way because the Nazis, following the Reich's defeats, forced prisoners to go out in the snow wearing next to nothing and in a state of severe malnutrition. Prisoners were marched without any rest stops and beaten or doused with ice-cold water to force them to keep moving when they collapsed from sheer exhaustion. Finally, the few who survived were taken by Soviet troops and incorporated into the Communist regime. Clara kept her life but lost her health: The suffering at the concentration camp left her with an incurable heart condition. Subsequently, Clara remarried a man named Seidmann, the former owner of a liquor distillery. The Communist government had expropriated his business and as a "big favor" had allowed him to live inside two small, dank rooms of the building where his business had once been. My daughter Lizy and I visited them there in 1962, when we traveled to Europe so she could meet her only surviving aunt and my *fräulein* Berta, both of whom were living under the Kremlin regime. Three years later, Clara died of poor health and a weak heart.

Of the three siblings, there was just my husband left, Adalbert Kaufmann. But who was this man, beyond this short description of his family? He was a discrete, unassuming man with a clear mind and sharp intelligence, and it was thanks to him that my parents and ourselves managed to escape the Nazi horror. To him I also owe the fact that I was able to build a solid family of my own after experiencing the material and spiritual precariousness of war. He is always in my thoughts and I am eternally grateful to him.

OLMÜTZ AND THE LEGACY

Two or three days after the wedding, I traveled to Olmütz with the papers showing that I was of age and, more importantly, that I was legally able to obtain Marko Heller's bequest, with the marriage certificate issued by the synagogue – back in those days, the civil marriage paperwork was handled and certified by the temple celebrating the religious ceremony, no matter what its creed. I traveled to Olmütz and returned to Prague the same day. After seeing the local juvenile court judge, I still had time to visit Aunt Alicia and my Grandmother Mathilde Goldschmidt, who was then living with her daughter. It was all very brief and intense.

Back in Prague, my husband was waiting for me at the station. It felt so strange to have a husband waiting for me! I suddenly had a wonderful feeling that I was no longer alone and even started to feel like I finally belonged to someone. I was returning with my trophy: an authorization to access the money left to me by my Uncle Marko. The money would be wired by the Olmütz juvenile court to the Böhmische Union Bank in Prague, Czechoslovakia's official banking institution. However, when I went to the Böhmische Union Bank, I was informed that the money had been deposited in a *Sperrkonto*, or blocked account. This meant that I could not freely access it, but would instead receive a weekly allowance equivalent to 200 dollars. The conditions also stipulated that any extraordinary expenses derived from professional services, as well as those relating to health, house moving, purchase of necessary goods and so on, would be paid for directly by the bank as long as proper receipts could be produced. This was not exactly what I had been expecting, but our situation did improve with this weekly stipend that, meager as it seemed, was still enough to live on in occupied Prague in 1940.

CONSTANTLY PERSECUTED

Days later, the management of the Hotel Flora, which had so kindly treated us to a fine lunch on our wedding day, informed us that we would no longer be allowed to stay at that establishment. The managers were acting on orders from higher authorities affecting all hotels. The Nazis decided that Jews could not live next to Christians inside the same hotel. We had to move, but where to? The Nazis were closing in on us, and it would be very hard to rent any apartment that required signing a lease. Fortunately, a relative of Aunt Alicia's named Alicia Morawetz recommended that I speak with a friend of hers, a Czech aristocrat who was being pressured by circumstances and by the Nazis to rent out part of her own spacious apartment. It was located in a building near the Hotel Alkron, on Štěpánská Street, just meters away from Václavské Náměstí (Wenceslas Square), an elegant area of Prague.

Frau Freund was a Jewish woman from Germany who had acquired Czech citizenship. She was also a truly insufferable person, but I managed to get her to rent us one room for my mother and another one for my husband and myself. She agreed on one condition: Only I would be allowed to use the kitchen. So we moved there, still waiting to hear about my father. My husband had sent the Gestapo a note from the Argentine Consulate requesting information about his whereabouts and suggesting that he should be released as there was no reason to deprive him of his freedom. Soon after that we received a letter from my father telling us he was being held at the Elisabeth Promenade prison in Vienna and that he was to be released within the week. We started feeling hopeful again and our outlook on life improved. Everything seemed to start making sense again.

Later, we learned that my father had indeed been released, but that he was so weak he could barely move and had gone to stay with his sister Grette. Grette was married to a man named Kaiser and would later be deported to Auschwitz, where she died. Under her care – which required many sacrifices as there was a shortage of everything in Vienna, especially food – my father recovered just enough to endure a train ride to Prague. We went to pick him up at the train station in a state of great agitation and excitement. It had been over a year since he had been surreptitiously arrested at the Hotel Flora and when we saw him walk down the steps of the train, we had trouble recognizing him. We were not sure whether that small, shrunken creature was really my father or not. He was extremely gaunt, had lost about 30 kilograms, and moved slowly, stumbling so often that he seemed like an old man even though he was only 45. He had grown weak after the forced labor he had been subjected to in Vienna, where he was made to load and unload coal, sweep the streets and scrub the sidewalks on his knees from daybreak to sundown – regardless of whether it was a sweltering day in August or an ice-cold, snowy winter's day. And all the while he had had to put up with all types of abuse because, as I said earlier, Jews were spat on, kicked around, barred from using the sidewalks and received insufficient amounts of food that was inedible in the first place; and that is without even mentioning many other wicked practices that were going on at the time.

We wept when we saw him in such a state. We hugged him and tried to sound encouraging, and I introduced him to my new husband, Adalbert

Kaufmann – whom he simply knew as the manager of the Hotel Flora. We tried to calm him and ourselves down and promised we would take good care of him and give him healthy food so he could get strong again soon. I knew that none of this would be easy because Prague also had food and fuel shortages, but right then my father needed our support more than actual knowledge about the harsh realities awaiting him. As if to make things even harder, when we arrived at the apartment where we rented rooms from Frau Freund, this lady informed us that she did not want a tenant who had been arrested by the Gestapo, because it made her fear for her own safety. She was adamant and she said that my father, at the very least, must leave immediately. She would only allow him to stay for lunch – it was noon – because she could see that he was exhausted and needed to eat.

I remember this as a moment of great despair during which we all stared at one another without knowing what to do. The regulations that had caused our eviction from the Hotel Flora were still in force, so it was useless to try to put my parents up at a different hotel. It was like being left out on the street. Once again we had to move; once again we had to look for a place to live, be lucky enough to find one, then to pack our belongings, move them to the new apartment, unpack, get used to our new surroundings, reorganize our lives, and start deciding which neighbors might be our allies and which our foes. Added to the bitterness caused by all this, there was also an inner weariness that was more spiritual than physical, which slowly took hold of us. It was a weariness constantly fueled by fear – a hidden, quiet, repressed kind of fear that made us scream on the inside but appear calm on the outside.

After the first moments of confusion, we tried to think straight. Serenity is always a source of good counsel and potential solutions, and given our emergency situation, we needed to find a solution fast. The answer to our problems came via my husband who, as usual, had remained calm throughout the entire incident. Years before, he had worked at the Hotel Axa, in Prague's second district, and he still had some friends there who held him in high esteem. Since it was not possible to handle this matter over the telephone – besides, the lines were barely working by then – my husband took a tram to the Hotel Axa and put the matter to his friends. Fortunately, they agreed to take in my parents, who moved to Pôric 32 that very same day, thus relieving the tension created by my father's arrival. In the meantime, Adalbert and I agreed to continue living in this bad-tempered woman's apartment.

Every day from then on, I fixed a meal in Frau Freund's kitchen, packed the food inside a box and took a tram to the Hotel Axa to bring my parents their lunch and dinner. I was doing it especially for my father, who needed my complete attention in order to get well again. It was a great physical effort for me, but the great love I felt for my father made me view it not as a sacrifice, but as a true act of filial love. Slowly, his health began to improve; little by little he recovered the strength he had lost in jail and every smile of his was a new triumph for me, a reward for my selfless dedication. During that period, I often thought about Berta and blessed her, because she had taught me how to be organized, how to select food items wisely so as to spend little money, how to combine items in ways that made them more filling, and how to cook and season them to produce healthy, appetizing dishes.

We were all living on the weekly stipend provided by my Uncle Marko Heller's bequest – which went mostly towards my parents' upkeep – and on the wages that my husband made at the Argentine Consulate. They were both small amounts, but I tried to make the best of it. In order to make the situation more tolerable, I started regarding it as a daily challenge, as a kind of game in which my opponent – daily subsistence – was a huge, powerful, menacing ogre, and the only weapon I had to fight it was my weekly stipend – a feeble sword that did not scare the ogre. This posed a great challenge since in such an ill-matched battle the sword would be useless unless I was able to use it cleverly. After the kind of easy living we had known in the past, it seemed unreal to have to endure this kind of hardship, yet such things happened during those times of war, especially to Jews living in Nazi-occupied countries.

I soon realized that it was morally difficult for my father to depend on me and my husband for a living. To someone who had always been the head of the family and the perfect embodiment of the protective father figure, it was tough to have to accept money from us. I decided to solve this problem before his suffering got any worse, because he had already suffered too much. Moreover, he was ill, and above everything else I loved and respected him deeply. So I asked him to help me manage the weekly stipend I was getting from the Böhmische Bank, arguing that of late I was starting to feel overwhelmed by so many responsibilities. From then on, he was the one who handed me the money I needed each day, not the other way around. And things did get better, even if it was nothing more than a game.

YEARNING FOR STABILITY

In the middle of all these troubles, I learned that there was a health center on the outskirts of Prague, in a place called Jíloviště, which had hot springs – something similar to what we would call a spa nowadays. At this center, a team of celebrated professionals offered guests physiotherapy, water therapy, kinesiology, physical exercise, massages, mineral baths and other wellness treatments as well as purifying diets. This, I thought, would be good for my father and would help restore his health. I found out – and this clinched it for me – that the Böhmische Bank would pay the cost of the clinic out of my blocked account because it was considered a medical service within the bounds of what my inheritance conditions stipulated. I did not hesitate to book two spots for my parents at the luxurious Jíloviště Institute, a place surrounded by beautiful gardens and lush forests where many Jews had already taken refuge. I thought my parents might run into friends and acquaintances there, and this would surely also make them feel better. Fortunately, everything worked out according to plan, and my parents were able to enjoy this piece of paradise for an entire month. It was far away from the war and their move was an unusually pleasant event in the midst of so much hardship.

In the meantime, feeling a bit less concerned, I decided to look for an apartment for my husband and myself. I also needed to find another place where my parents might live when they got back from the Jíloviště Institute. Sometimes, I still entertained hopes that one day we would all live in peace again, but at the same time, I felt like I was after something unattainable. My expectations filled me with guilt and seemed excessively ambitious. All I was dreaming of was a comfortable home where I might lead a normal life, free of constant emotional shocks. It was a normal human desire, but the state of personal devaluation that the Nazi regime was reducing us to made happiness and well-being seem like things that only Germans, and specifically Nazis, had a right to. That's what things had come down to.

Finding strength where there was almost none, I began the apartment search. I found a home for my husband and myself on Lobkowitz Náměstí. It was a modest, unfurnished apartment, which meant we had to buy furniture with money from my blocked account. It had a tiny entrance hall, a bedroom, an ample bathroom, a basic kitchen and a large, pretty balcony. Later, I found another apartment on Libická Street, very near the Hotel Flora, which I rented for my parents. It was an attic studio apartment with one room, a kitchenette and a pantry. There was a washbasin but the toilet was a shared one, out in the hallway. Although I knew this would be inconvenient for my parents, I figured that the good location would make up for this deficiency. I was fully aware that, once again, I was yielding to the devastating Nazi plan to make us feel unworthy of creature comforts, but I could either accept the reality or succumb to it. When my parents returned from Jíloviště – my father looking significantly better – they settled in this apartment and I might say that we all began to enjoy a much yearned for period of peace, even if our living conditions kept getting worse.

SHORTAGE AND RATIONING

The rationing of provisions and other staple items imposed by the German occupiers not only continued, but got stricter every day. It was impossible to buy food without the corresponding voucher, and obtaining these vouchers, which were handed out by local authorities in each district, was an added adventure in the middle of so many difficulties. The vouchers for Jews had a "J" stamped in one corner to identify the bearer. This meant that we could only purchase products within specific time frames, and many businesses happened to close their doors at those times. Often, we managed to buy what we needed by giving up some of our belongings, especially if they were of some value, and often a good rug ended up as payment for a few eggs, vegetables and milk products. We were allowed to buy one egg every 15 days. Potatoes were a feast, and when we did eat them, we carefully saved the peels so we could cook them the next day, when they would be all we had for lunch, and possibly dinner as well. There was no meat and no milk, or only occasionally, and certainly not for Jews, not even for the children. We lived on dried foods – beans, chick peas, lentils – all of very poor quality – gray-black noodles, bread and water. We sporadically got our hands on some food with more calories, which was especially necessary when winter came round. This poor nutrition slowly manifested itself in dry skin, dental problems and brittle nails that were deformed and scaly; sparse, unhealthy-looking hair that kept falling out without growing back; swollen bellies and frequent bone fractures; states of fatigue and depression; and insomnia or sleepiness caused by a lack of either the strength or the willpower to face the harsh realities of the waking hours.

One day, my husband brought me a voucher to buy two kilos of rice or dried foods, given to him by Ambassador Brunel. The ambassador had not used it himself because he could not find anyone to sell him rice and he was not interested in any of the other products that could be obtained with this voucher. I went to a very small and poor-looking establishment located on the ground floor of the building where my parents lived. It was run by a good woman with whom we had established a pleasant relationship as clients. She always wore a pointed woolen hat with a pompom on the tip, which is why my father referred to her in family conversations as *Frau Zipfelhauben*, something like "Mrs. Pointy Hat." It was a funny nickname that my father used kindly to express appreciation, because this woman often put aside for us a bit of margarine or cheese, both very precious goods back then. When I told Frau Zipfelhauben that I had this voucher and began selecting some of the most common dried foods, she gently asked me whether I would not prefer some rice. "Rice! Rice? Did you say rice?" I asked in a fluster. "Yes, rice. But lower your voice! Nobody thinks that such an insignificant establishment as this one could possibly have rice. I keep it for my clients, but only the ones I trust."

I returned home as if I were transporting gold, walking at a fast clip and turning every so often to check that nobody was going to take my treasure away. I finally arrived home with my two kilos of rice, flushed and triumphant. But when my husband returned from work, he said that if I had managed to buy rice with the ambassador's voucher, then the rice belonged to him, since he had given us the voucher precisely because he could not find rice himself. Were there to be just one single grain of rice available in all of Prague, this single grain should go to him as the rightful owner of the voucher, he said. I thought I was going to die. I was hungry — hungry for something substantial and appetizing, and now that I had it, I was losing it. I pleaded, I cried, I negotiated: "One kilo for him, one for us," I implored. "No," was the reply. "Half a kilo for us," I insisted. But it was useless. My husband's faultless upbringing and strict, unshakeable ethics had already decided the matter: The two kilos of rice went to the ambassador, who never found out about my pleading and negotiating.

AN EXCITING ANNOUNCEMENT

While all this was going on, our family had gradually stopped practicing its religion and traditions. The insecurity all around us, my father's repeated arrests, our various moves, Aunt Alicia's unsuccessful trip to Paris, my own failed engagement to Willy Groak and my marriage to Adalbert Kaufmann – all of which took place in the space of just two years – had had such an emotional impact on us that religious practice had been pushed into the background. However, my father continued to observe the smoking ban on Saturdays, an attitude of marginal significance but proved his desire to respect the precepts handed down from generation to generation, and to honor the promise to uphold these values that he had made to his dying grandmother at age 18.

On December 24, Christmas Eve 1940, I felt a sickness that I had never felt before. After nearly a month without improvement, I went to see a doctor and found out I was pregnant. The news filled me with joy. I suddenly felt a deep-rooted happiness that I wanted to share with the world. I wanted to scream it out from the rooftops. The first person to find out was my husband, and then I told my parents. But unlike me, they all seemed quite concerned, and my father said with great alarm: "How can you bring a human being into the world at such a horrible time? Don't you know that Jews are being sent away to the gas chambers?"[12] His words were so harsh and so unexpected that, for the first time in my life, I talked back to my father: "I am going to have this baby and I am going to fight for him. If he must die in the gas chamber, then we will die together, because I will never leave him. But I *will* experience the joy and happiness of holding a child in my arms, and I will fight to the end to make it so. If they come for him, we will jump out of a seventh-floor window together so they can't take him away from me."

12 Editorial note: At the end of 1940, there were no gas chambers and Jews were not sent to death camps. The first death camp began its operations on December 8, 1941. The author probably mentioned here what she learned later on.

A NEW PROBLEM

Before fleeing from Austria my father had entrusted a work colleague named Egon Winkler with a pearl necklace and a diamond ring that he had given my mother as gifts. It turned out that Egon Winkler had ties to the Nazis and he reported the items to the Gestapo, which considered any jewels belonging to Jews as part of the German state's assets and should be declared. Not doing so was tantamount to stealing from the Reich. The legal proceedings sparked by the report took shape in late February 1941, when my father received a summons from the Deutsches Amtsgericht Prag, the German tribunal in Prague, which was located in the area of Bubentsch, on Unter den Kastanien Street 24, the same department where I had been declared of marriageable age in May 1940. I accompanied my father to court every time he had to show up, until a sentence was finally handed down: He would have to serve a three-month prison sentence.

We returned home knowing that in just a few days a notice would arrive instructing him to report to the prison where he was to serve his sentence. Weighed down by so much madness and feeling defeated by so much unfair persecution, my father sobbed that when the time came to go to jail, he would simply take his own life. I knew that these were not empty words. My father was overwhelmed, broken, defeated. It was understandable that he no longer felt strong enough to face the torture of prison, especially for such an unfair reason, and that he no longer felt the strength to go on living. It hurt me to see him this way, so different from the person he had once been. His enthusiasm, his fortitude and his optimism were nothing but memories now. So I promised my father that I would do my utmost to ensure he would not have to go to jail again, and even took the risk of assuring him that he would never again be a prisoner.

I was not feeling my best either. I was into the third month of my pregnancy and was suffering from stomach problems and spells of nausea that caused unpleasant and uncontrollable diarrhea. I generally felt really bad in the mornings, but I had decided that I would have this child, and I had to be strong, very strong, to sustain this being that was growing inside me just as I had to sustain that other being whom I loved so much, and who was standing there by my side, dying of sadness. Both were weak and needed me. And I...well, I pretended to be strong. I asked questions, reflected on the answers, investigated my choices and weighed my options. I finally found out that if an official doctor certified that my father really had a heart condition – which he did – he could obtain a 30-day stay of execution from the court.

I managed to talk to a Czechoslovak doctor who was authorized to issue these certificates. He was not a Nazi and, after listening to my story, he gave me the piece of paper that would postpone my father's imprisonment for a month. After the first month, I went back to see the same doctor, who issued another certificate. We did this every 30 days, and each renewal sapped our remaining strength because of the agony of not knowing whether the stay would be accepted or not. And when it was accepted, another 30-day period opened up before us that we knew would go by at lightning speed, plunging us once again into more despair. We knew that the day's victory would not deliver us from having to fight a similar battle 30 days later, and in between battles my father was being consumed by stress, while I had many sleepless nights as my belly grew to accommodate my developing child.

All the while, my husband was trying to obtain, through his job at the Argentine Consulate, legal permission for my parents to leave Czechoslovakia. But because of the German court's ruling against my father, which was still suspended, it was impossible to get him a legal visa. We clearly needed to find another way to get them out of this insane situation. We knew there was someone in Prague who helped Jews escape Czechoslovakia by providing them with passports and this was exactly what we needed. We knew we would have to pay the equivalent of 70,000 to 80,000 dollars for this service, which was approximately all that was left in my blocked bank account. So I went to see this man and asked him to get me the necessary passports or documents to take my parents out of Nazi-occupied territory. He would be able to take the money directly out of my bank account thanks to his contacts in the German government. While the papers were being drawn up, however, we needed yet another deferral of my father's prison sentence. It was the seventh one, the last one allowed by law. But when I went to see the doctor who had always been so helpful, he said that he could no longer give my father a certificate because new regulations had gone into effect and breaking them could cost him his life. It was a tough blow. I was already eight months' pregnant and could not stand the idea that my father might be in jail when my child was born. But the really crucial thing was that my father must be ready to leave as soon as the passports arrived, so he and my mother could get away from the Nazis.

I gathered up my courage and went to Gestapo headquarters. I asked to speak to someone in charge and explained that I needed my father to be with me until my child was born. I promised I would take him to prison myself as soon as I got out of the hospital. If I failed to do so, they could take me as a hostage. The official who heard me out said I was lucky to be speaking to him, because his wife was expecting their first child around the same time as I was expecting mine, and he would grant me the permission I requested for my father. But he made it very clear that I should take him to prison no later than five days after the birth, which I expected to be between September 8 and 10.

FINALLY, SOME GOOD NEWS

Unexpectedly, on August 31, 1941, my parents were informed that their passports were ready and that on September 2 they should board the last train taking Jews out of Czechoslovakia to Spain via Berlin. The cost of this service had been deducted from my blocked bank account. From this moment on, I would no longer receive a weekly stipend because the money from my Uncle Marko Heller's inheritance had run out, meaning that my account was empty and therefore closed. From now on, my husband and I would have to live on the money he made at the consulate, a fact that he accepted graciously and with true generosity. This was a significant setback for us, coming as it did just a few days before our baby was due. But I had managed to save my parents. God would provide for our own needs later on.

We took my parents to Wilsonovo nádraží, Prague's main train station. They had hardly any luggage with them, just a few personal effects: some clothes, toiletries and medicines. Before their departure, we learned that Argentina's Foreign Affairs Ministry in Buenos Aires had just granted them the desired authorization to legally enter the country. It was a relief to know that they would be welcome there. However, although I did not say so out loud, I was deathly afraid that they might not make it to their destination. They had to travel through Berlin before heading for Spain and this filled me with fear.

The train left at 11 in the morning with very few passengers on board.

We said our goodbyes quickly, holding back our emotions. We raised our hands and waved goodbye discreetly, fearfully, prudently. It seemed like we had to conceal their departure, in case the wolves realized at the last minute that a prey was slipping out of their clutches — or in case they regretted having been so "magnanimous" as to allow my parents to escape that mortal trap. The pain of being separated from my father was too strong and I fainted. Luckily, my husband caught me, lifted me in his arms and carried me to the home of some friends, named Altschul, who lived near the station and who were kind enough to help us. Years later we were to learn that Mr. Altschul, a multimillionaire banker, and his entire family perished inside a gas chamber at a death camp.

Once I had recovered from my fainting spell, we went home. It was hot and my belly felt heavy, even though it was smaller than that of a woman about to give birth. But my soul felt greatly relieved. I prayed, asking God to protect my parents and help them reach Argentina safe and sound. That night, when the tension created by my parents' departure had subsided, I lay down to relax for a while. By then I had recovered from the physical effort of going to the station on that hot, muggy day that weighed me down even more than my belly, and also from the emotional distress of seeing my parents go. As I lay back, I turned on the radio to listen to the BBC, the station that was banned by the Nazis. The first thing I heard was that the Allies were at that precise moment bombing Berlin, and that the air raid was the biggest one to date.

I thought I would go mad. The air raid described by the BBC was tremendous and my parents were probably already in Berlin; in fact, they could be dead by now. My God! I began trembling; first I felt cold, then I was boiling hot. I wanted to cry but could not. By turns I screamed, implored and whimpered. I was just one step away from insanity. Keeping calm as usual, my husband sought a way to relieve my pain. And, as usual, he found it. Since private telephones were no longer working, he called Ambassador Brunel from a public phone on the ground floor of the building where we lived, which was a risky thing to do as Jews were barred from using it. He asked the ambassador whether it was possible to know what was really going on in Berlin and what had happened to the small group of travelers who had left Prague that morning for the city. Ambassador Brunel called the Argentine Embassy in Berlin and managed to have them locate my parents. Not only did we hear about them; we were actually able to speak to them the next morning from my husband's office. I was able to hear my father's voice, then my mother's. They were alive. The bombing had destroyed almost the entire city, but they were alright and they would resume their journey to Spain that afternoon. Now I was getting all worked up with the joy of knowing they were alive. I thanked God, I thanked Ambassador Brunel, I thanked my husband and I blessed them all. I cried and I laughed, I laughed and I cried. I was very agitated and that was not good for me, so close to my due date.

THE BIRTH OF MY SON

Two days later, Berta showed up in Prague to help me with my delivery. Before leaving and despite the slump he was going through, my father had worked to make sure that I would be cared for and in good company before and after giving birth.

Berta's arrival made me feel safe and strong and it was a real joy to see her. However, I must confess that neither she, nor I, had the slightest clue about childbirth, and as a result, when my placenta broke on September 7 and I started losing amniotic fluid, she insisted that I had to walk a lot – inside my room, of course, because it was nighttime. Fortunately, I had a bad cold and did not feel like walking. By early next morning, I required medical attention. We had no money left, since all our savings had been spent on my parents' journey and we had no vehicle to get to the hospital. Fortunately, the commercial attaché at the Argentine Consulate was kind enough to offer us his car. I was admitted to a militarized hospital whose maternity ward had a special area for Jewish women. I was left there all alone, because they did not allow anyone in with the patients, so my husband and Berta could not be by my side, even though I wanted them to be there so badly.

When we arrived at the hospital, I was asked about the purpose of my visit. I weighed 46 kilograms and the baby was small, so they had not even realized I was pregnant. But I was already in labor with frequent and intense contractions. The pain gradually increased, but the frequency of the contractions did not, so there was no indication that delivery was anywhere near. I suffered in complete ignorance of the entire process, which had never been explained to me or even insinuated, due to the kind of upbringing I'd

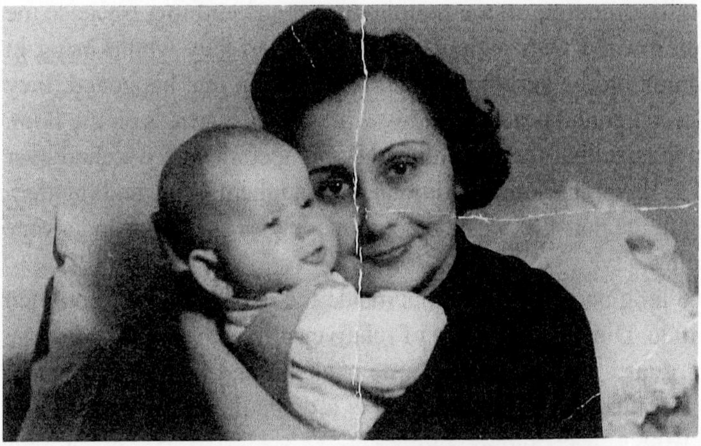

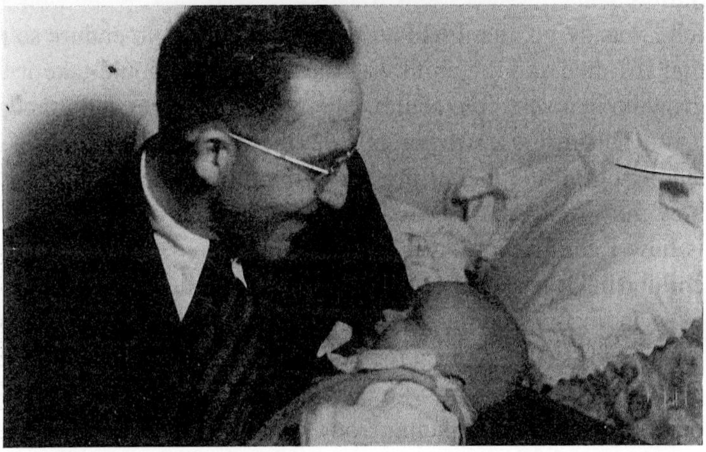

Happy moments during hard times.

had. At home, these things had never been discussed, at least not in front of me.

It was almost 40 hours before the baby was born. I had been placed on a stretcher inside a cold, bare delivery room. From the stretcher where I lay nearly paralyzed by pain, the ceiling was a white rectangle, which my eyes scanned again and again, looking for an image, a shadow, a reflection that might distract me from so much suffering. I needed something, no matter how small, to hold on to; something in the middle of so much nothing. Because the hospital was overcrowded with patients, every so often they would bring in a non-Jewish woman on the verge of giving birth. When that happened, they took me off the stretcher and practically threw me onto a mattress on the floor. But I want to emphasize that the Czech nurses and doctors who watched over me were as kind as the precarious conditions allowed them to be, and the doctor who helped with the delivery was a prestigious Jewish specialist and a very decent human being.

I spent two long and painful nights inside the delivery room, hounded by pain and solitude. During a moment of relative calm, I managed to get the woman standing guard at the door to come near me and listen to my plea: I wanted to see my husband. I knew this was a difficult and compromising request, but the woman was understanding and put herself at risk by allowing him to come into the room. When he was finally by my side, I told him that I felt I was dying, that I had no more strength left to endure so much pain, and that if I died and the child was born alive, he should take it to Argentina to grow up in a vast, free country alongside his father and grandparents.

During those two nights, I was the involuntary witness of several births — simply out of the fact of my being there in the room — and I saw and heard how the women suffered as they brought their children into the world. That is how I confirmed that the biblical mandate of "great will be your pain in childbirth" is true every time, regardless of religion, skin color or wealth. And even if, in the middle of my own pain, I rebelliously wondered about the reasons for such a biblical mandate, I found solace in hearing each and every newborn utter the same whimper, the same cry that has surely come with the birth of every human being from time immemorial. After the crying would come a moment of nearly complete silence, and then the whispering voice of the mother saying sweet words when she was shown her baby and the two met, ready to undertake the journey of life together.

It was past noon on Wednesday, September 10, 1941 when the labor pains started to speed up. The contractions were coming in quick succession now, almost without pause, and they were increasingly painful. Even though I did not get an anesthetic, at times I briefly lost consciousness. At one point I opened my eyes and saw a number of faces staring at me from above, as if peering out from a balcony. Silhouetted against that bare ceiling that had offered me nothing but the cold landscape of its mute whiteness the day before, these faces seemed like a garland of strange eyes outlining an oval in the clear sky. It turned out that these people were the pupils of the head of the obstetrics department who had come to watch the deliveries as part of a practical training session. This is a regular practice at hospitals and not very pleasant for the patients, but at that point and after so much suffering, nothing mattered anymore.

The delivery was normal and took place at two in the afternoon. After hearing the voices that talked me through the process and the noise of surgical instruments came the sound of my baby crying, and after the crying came a wonderful feeling when a pair of hands, human and generous, placed the small, trembling body in the hollow of my shoulder, near my cheek. My son Carlos was born and his arrival made the rest of the world suddenly stop existing. I forgot about the war, forgot about Hitler, forgot about Nazism. I forgot that my father was far away. The physical suffering had ended and I had already forgotten it, and the indescribable joy that overwhelmed me was a sign that my son and I were also embarking on the journey of life together. I must admit that Carlos was not a beautiful newborn. The long hours of suffering had left their mark on his tiny face, still humid against my cheek, and his open eyes were red and swollen. But I was so overjoyed at seeing him by my side and feeling the warmth of his body, that I thought he was the most gorgeous child in the entire world. It was as though the skies had opened up and all kinds of heavenly blessings were being visited on me.

I was taken to a small room with barely enough space for the beds in which three young women — aged 15, 17 and 18 — were lying. We all knew without a shadow of a doubt what our own end might be, but because we had just given birth to our children, we were sustained as if by a magic force. Two of them had had girls and the third, whose married name was also Kaufmann, had had a boy. I was given her bed when she and her child were sent home. Sometime later, I found out that both had been deported to Theresienstadt and were never heard from again. My husband arrived some time later, because the moment he found out that we were both safe and sound he ran to the post office to send my parents a telegram informing them of the birth of their grandson Carlos. The telegram was allowed to go through because it was signed by the Argentine ambassador. It was addressed to my father, and said: "Your daughter Ilse and your grandson Carlos in perfect health. Congratulations. Carlos

Brunel." My husband brought me three beautiful roses and when he saw his son he was truly moved. He looked fascinated, proud and happy.

Carlos was taken to a nursery of sorts where there were only two cribs for three babies. From my room I could hear all three of them crying, but I could immediately tell whether Carlos was one of them or whether he was quiet, perhaps asleep. Already from those early days and throughout my son's life, communication between the two of us was incredibly strong; I might even say indestructible, unbreakable. On the same day that Carlos was born, and almost at the same time, there was a baby girl born to the Italian ambassador's wife. Sadly, the mother died during childbirth. The news was sad and shocking. Later, we learned that the little one needed breast milk and that it was not to be found anywhere, so I offered to nurse her since I had enough milk for my son and for her as well. But racial laws prohibited a Jewish woman from nursing a Christian child and the poor little creature died. Perhaps if those evil laws had not existed, the baby would have lived.

We named our son Carlos in honor of the Argentine Ambassador, Carlos Brunel, who had helped us so much and who wanted to be the child's godfather. The day that he came to meet his godson, the baby was wearing a little smock that I had knitted myself and which, due to my poor knitting skills, had come out with one sleeve longer than the other. This led the ambassador to assume that his godson was born with a deformity. When my husband explained that the "deformity" was caused by my lack of knitting abilities, they both had a good laugh. A few days later, the ambassador sent us a beautiful baby kit which he had ordered from Switzerland as a gift to his godson. The layette naturally included smocks with sleeves of matching length.

Six or seven days later, I was sent home. A nurse carried the baby while I leaned on my husband's arm. Waiting at the door was Ambassador Brunel inside his black Cadillac, which had a small Argentine flag on one side and the Nazi swastika on the other, in accordance with existing regulations. The ambassador took Carlos in his arms and said a few words in Spanish that I did not understand, but which my husband later translated for me: "I wish for you to be a free man in a vast, free country and I wish for you to grow up and make your parents happy and your future country proud. God bless you." And with a smile, he added: "And may you always travel in a Cadillac."

THAT OLD ACQUAINTANCE, FEAR

When the car started moving, I noticed that several pedestrians were wearing something that looked like a badge on the left side of their chest. I saw Jewish traits on their faces and asked fearfully what this thing pinned to their clothes meant. It was the Star of David, the symbol of Judaism, which had been sewn onto a piece of yellow cloth along with the word "Jude," and from that day on it was mandatory for anyone of Jewish origin to wear it. I felt a wave of terror wash over me. I sensed that something awful was about to happen. From that moment on, we would all be singled out as targets for aggression, offence and the violation of our rights; and besides that – which was already too much – we would be easily identifiable to the Nazis, whose thirst for blood and revenge – revenge for what? – could never be quenched.

A shiver went down my spine. It was fear once again – the same fear that was always there in the back of our minds, and whose presence always dampened any spark of joy, any glimpse of happiness, even this fleeting moment when I was going home with a child in my arms, feeling safe and happy inside an official vehicle, protected by the flag of a neutral country and calm because my husband, though Jewish, was exempt from having to wear the yellow badge because he was a staff member of the Argentine Consulate in Prague. Besides, my parents were safe and on their way to this land of promise, and Berta was waiting at home with beautiful flowers for me, ready to help me care for the baby. Everything seemed to point to a new period of serenity up ahead, but once again, this hateful feeling of fear was taking my happiness away. How many more times would it torture me with its unexpected appearances? How much longer would we be its plaything?

For the next few days, I was busy organizing my son's life and did not even step out of the house. His hygiene and eating schedule – which were entirely my responsibility as I was breastfeeding him – together with my lack of experience in caring for a baby and the immense joy I was feeling, all contributed to distract me. But one day, I suddenly remembered the prison postponement I had obtained for my father. I remembered that I had promised to take him there myself once my child was born and if I failed to do so, I would be held prisoner in his place. My father was no longer in Prague and they would look for me and find me. I was suddenly scared to death.

Nazi laws against Jews were becoming increasingly cruel with each passing day. They were also cruel against the Czechoslovakians, who suffered enormously under German occupation. We were only allowed to buy food and other necessary items at certain times, which generally coincided with the establishments' closing hours. We were barred from using elevators, even in emergency situations, so when air raid sirens went off we had to grope our way down the stairs in the darkness, lighting up the steps with a weak flashlight. Since our apartment was on the seventh floor, it was hard work rushing down the stairs in the middle of that darkness, carrying a baby in my arms and feeling understandably nervous because of the dangerous situation. We were also barred from taking refuge with the other people in the basement, which was a bunker of sorts. Jews were not entitled to protection, so we simply went into a room that was located next to the doorman's housing quarters, and which his wife, Marenca Swoboda, secretly let us into for safety. It was in this small room that this good woman allowed me to keep Carlos' baby carriage; otherwise I would have had to carry it up and down seven flights of stairs every time I went out with the child. One day, Marenca mysteriously disappeared and we later learned that she had been sent to Auschwitz and died there. In those days, under the Nazi regime, helping Jews was an unpardonable offence.

Prague, like Austria before it, had also enforced the prohibition for Jews to use the sidewalks, so we had to walk on the road. We were not allowed to use public phones and the private lines inside our homes had been disconnected. Jewish children could not play in parks, much less with children of other religions. There was a shortage of food, and in our case there was a shortage of vouchers, which were always handed out at inconvenient locations where we had to endure long lines, generally out in the open. Life had become a permanent state of suffering. Because the public parks were off-limits to us, on sunny days I used to take Carlos to the old Jewish cemetery that is still next to the Old and New Synagogue, and which had already become a monument, even back then, since no more burials were taking place. I had to walk nearly an hour to get there — on the road, not the sidewalk — but at least I felt at ease, because other Jewish mothers were playing there with their own children. I have often wondered whether it is possible to measure the evil inside the souls of people who could enforce such unspeakable rules as to prohibit children from playing in a park just because they were Jewish. I never did find the answer. Is it not the most normal thing in the world for a child to play in the park?

On the days when I went to the park with Carlos, my husband made a thousand recommendations about how I had to be careful, stay alert, avoid certain areas and not be late back. He was very uneasy while we awaited authorization to travel to Argentina, because the situation was growing more dangerous by the day. We knew that many Jews – sometimes entire families – were being deported to a concentration camp located in the Polish town of Oświęcim – whose translation into German is Auschwitz – near the Vistula River, 30 kilometers south of Katowice. It was presumed that these people would never return.

On October 20 of that year, 1941, we received a shocking telegram from the Argentine Foreign Affairs Ministry informing us that our visas were being cancelled because of the birth of our child. We felt enormous despair, but my husband quickly regained his composure, and drawing on his practical sense and habitual optimism, he sent an urgent letter to Buenos Aires along with a note from the ambassador stressing the growing danger and the need for us to obtain a family visa so we could leave Europe as soon as possible. The reply we longed for came sooner rather than later and the Argentine Foreign Affairs Ministry informed us that a new, special authorization had been issued so that my husband, my child and I could travel to Buenos Aires on Argentine passports. However, it was clearly indicated that these documents did not grant us actual citizenship.

AUNT ALICIA AND THE SAFE-DEPOSIT BOX

Our anxiety had subsided and we began planning our trip to freedom. We knew that nothing would come easy and that our money, which was already inadequate for daily living, would be greatly insufficient for such a long journey, especially with such a small child. But we were optimistic and ready to take on whatever problems came our way, trusting that we would be able to solve them as we went along.

We were in the middle of our plans when we received news from Aunt Alicia in early December of that same year, 1941. She had been summoned by the Union Bank, on the Reich's orders, to open up the safe-deposit box under her name, which she had rented following the advice of her boyfriend, bank director Otto Sametz, when she moved from Olmütz to Prague, in case the Germans occupied Moravia. It was obvious that the goal of the summons was to expropriate the goods that she kept inside the box; that is to say, the numerous pieces of fine silverware whose weight exceeded 50 kilos and whose value ran into thousands of dollars.

My husband consulted Ambassador Brunel over what steps might be taken to conserve these assets that, we knew, could save our lives in the future, either by trading them in for food or using them as a means for securing safe conduct. The result was that the Argentine Embassy sent an official note to the Union Bank informing its officials that a certain amount of the items inside the box belonged to Mr. Adalbert Kaufmann and his wife, Edith Ilse Kaufmann. Fortunately, my husband's links to this diplomatic mission bore fruit and the bank let us retrieve the items on the list attached to the embassy note – nearly half of the total – and allowed Aunt Alicia and ourselves to do a little trading, which, although dangerous, was vital during those unhinged times under the Nazi regime. Aunt Alicia's trip from Olmütz to Prague to see to this business was very short because she was in very poor health and weak, and even breathing tired her out. As compensation for her efforts, she had the great, if only fleeting, joy of meeting my son Carlos, who was then a beautiful three-month-old baby.

A KNOCK AT OUR DOOR

Around 60 days had gone by since Aunt Alicia had returned to Olmütz and things appeared to have quieted down, when suddenly a Czechoslovakian police officer came knocking at our door, bringing me a summons from the Gestapo. It was early April 1942, and the moment I had been dreading was finally upon me. The summons had to do with the promise I had made the German official to take my father to jail after giving birth to my child, so he could serve the sentence that had been postponed time and again thanks to the medical certificates. While he handed me the summons, the Czech officer kept looking at my son, who was five months old at the time, and repeating: "Poor little orphan, poor little orphan!"

That night felt like it would never end. I was panicking at the thought that I would have to face the Gestapo the following morning. Thinking that I would probably never come back home again made me feel defeated, horrified and heartbroken. I would never see my son again and that was the worst part of all. In despair, I paced our small apartment, stopping every so often in front of Carlos' crib to caress him as he slept peacefully, looking the very image of innocence as all sleeping children do. I wondered what the Gestapo would ask me the next day, and I shook with fear. I said goodbye to my child and wept in despair. I went back to bed hoping to get some sleep, but jumped up again as if ejected from the mattress by a spring and started pacing again. I uselessly wished I could make time stand still and prevent that dreaded morning from arriving, or else speed things up to make everything happen as quickly as possible and be done with the hours of anguish and cruel uncertainty that were eating me up from the inside.

As was to be expected, the next morning arrived at its own pace. It neither came early because of my impatience nor late because of my fear. I fearlessly – almost aggressively, I would say – pinned the Star of David to my coat and walked to the Gestapo offices, since I could not afford the tramway fare. It was not a cold day, but I felt cold. I walked faster in order to make more of a physical effort, and that made me feel better. When I arrived at the headquarters I was no longer tortured by the cold, but I felt nauseated at the sight of that sordid building, which had once been the beautiful home of the Petschek Bank, now expropriated to make room for the Gestapo offices. The Petschek family's mansion on Unter den Kastanien Street 24 had also been expropriated and now housed the National Court of First Instance that had granted me my proof-of-age papers.

I was taken to a room where an officer from the SS subjected me to an interrogation during which I was made to stand while he sat comfortably, at times asking me questions and at times ignoring me completely as he saw to other matters. A period of time that seemed like an eternity elapsed, while the following dialogue took place over and over: "Where is your father?" yelled the officer. "I don't know, because when I went to pick him up to bring him here, he was not home and nobody could tell me where he might be," I answered firmly, trying to sound convincing. "You're lying!" he hollered at the top of his lungs. I felt like dying. But the many vicissitudes that I had dealt with in recent times made me strong enough not to break down. "You're lying!" he yelled again. "Do you know what will happen to you if you keep lying?" And he ended this threat by staring into my eyes as if he were going to devour me.

I certainly knew what he was talking about. At that time, many Jewish families were receiving summonses requesting them to show up on the first floor of the building located on Phillip-de-Monte-Gasse 15 early the next day, generally at around seven in the morning. From there they were taken to Theresienstadt and then deported to Auschwitz or one of the other, equally fearsome concentration and extermination camps. "Actually, I do know," I replied. "I know exactly what you are talking about. But aren't you demanding that I tell you the truth? Well, that is what I'm doing. Or should I make something up to please you? You must understand, Sir, that I am merely following your orders," I said over and over, emphasizing the word "sir" and deliberately using the term "orders" to flatter his ego, even as my knees shook. "Who helped your father get out of Prague?" he exclaimed, moving on to another topic. "I don't know. I don't know whether my father is or isn't in Prague. You must understand that I don't know where my father is right now." "Do you know an engineer named Bestiak?" he yelled. "I don't know who that is," I replied, even though I knew he was the man to whom we had paid 80,000 dollars in order to get my parents out of Europe. "I don't know who this person is, I have never heard that name." "He told me he knows you," he said. "I don't know who that person is," I repeated.

Even though I had been raised by my parents to always tell the truth, I grabbed at my only chance of salvation in the midst of so many changes to all the things we lived by: I lied. I lied and I backed up my lies as if they were the purest truth on the face of the earth. At that precise moment, when the officer seemed on the verge of collapsing out of sheer indignation, a door opened and a uniformed woman came in. "There is a man outside who is not Jewish and who says he is this bitch's husband," she said. Since my husband was exempt from wearing the Star of David, the woman assumed he was not Jewish and did not ask him any questions. My husband introduced himself as the Secretary of the Argentine Consulate in Prague and showed the officer the letter from the German Foreign Affairs Ministry, which we had received two days earlier, indicating that we were authorized to leave German territory, and which was dated and stamped in Berlin. "Are you her husband?" the officer enquired suspiciously. "Yes, I am," my husband replied laconically. As a sign that the officer accepted this statement as truth, he turned to me and for the first time, said: "Take a seat, Madam."

My husband's credentials were enough for the screaming SS official to bring his voice down several decibels and adopt a slightly more civilized tone, inasmuch as his brutal training allowed. However, his harshness persisted until the end of the interview. Although he became less aggressive when he saw my husband's credentials, his inner desire to hurt had not been assuaged. That much was obvious. He looked like a hound that had been deprived of its last exterminating bite.

We walked out of that dismal building – once a source of admiration because of its splendid appearance – into a sunny day. Needless to say, my knees were knocking and I could hardly walk. My whole body shook as a shiver ran down my spine. I felt born again and my savior was my husband who, like David before Goliath, had been able to aim his blow just right to bring down the giant. Like David, he was the most humble of his father's children, and like David he had carefully selected the simplest weapon to defeat the arrogant Philistine in an uneven match. My gratitude to him is boundless, and I still feel it as strongly today as I did back then.

Returning home and finding my son safe and happy made me feel like I was in heaven. I took Carlos in my arms, hugged and kissed him, and told him a thousand times that I would always be with him and we would never be separated. He looked at me with his shiny eyes and, since he had begun babbling, it seemed like he was carrying out a conversation with me as he made funny sounds with his mouth. In my motherly fantasies, I fancied that he could understand what I said and so I only told him sweet things, promising him a successful future and assuring him I would always be by his side to help and protect him.

Meanwhile, war had spread across the world into an inferno fueled by hatred, vindictiveness and acts of revenge. Europe, Japan, Russia, part of Africa and the Middle East were being consumed by it, as were thousands upon thousands of innocent souls. A world of hope and possibilities for humankind was reduced to ashes, leaving behind a trail of pain that is still not gone. War was everywhere and, to a greater or lesser extent, it affected and hurt us all. All the ingredients of war were there: the concentration and extermination camps with their gas chambers; the cities, great and small, heartlessly razed by land or air raids; dead and crippled people by the thousands; children turned into orphans and deprived of their childhood; a future full of uncertainty for everyone; the massacres, the cold, the hunger, the fear.... These were then, as they are still now, the necessary ingredients of any war; and this was a ferocious war indeed.

I remember those harsh winter days in Prague when there was no heating fuel and how I changed the baby's diapers under a duvet that I held up with my head while I pulled off the dirty diaper and put on the clean one as fast as I could to prevent him from getting cold; but despite my efforts, the poor little thing cried from the cold and many times his skin turned purplish. Since we also lacked electric light, I used a flashlight that would often fall due to the baby's kicking, either in play or when he felt smothered under the duvet, or else when I knocked it down myself in my haste to change him — all of which made the whole operation a stressful ordeal for him as well as for me. After this struggle with the diapers, the duvet, the flashlight and the cold, I wrapped my son up and placed him against my breast, hoping that the milk would provide enough nourishment to bring some heat back into his little body. But I had my doubts, because on many days all I had to eat was a plate of darkish, flavorless noodles, lentils or boiled beans. The shortage of food was wreaking havoc on us and on top of all these deprivations we could only prepare meals when there was electricity — between midnight and two in the morning, from May to September.

As soon as winter set in, the water froze because of the intense cold and the pipes burst inside the buildings, leaving people without water first, and then, when the temperature rose and the ice thawed, causing the water to seep between the cracks and create damp spots on floors, walls, furniture and anything else that happened to be near the burst pipe. The damage was repaired by tying rags around the affected area, which only just managed to prevent the rushing water from splashing everywhere. The residual dampness, which soon became ugly and foul-smelling, left a green mark behind, like a brushstroke of sadness. We sometimes obtained and used methylated spirit to light a small, very basic kind of heater, but all fuel was in great demand and this made life at home a constant struggle. Even though there was no actual fighting going on in Prague, we lived in a state of all-out war. Until one experiences this kind of thing, it is impossible to understand.

A MAJOR INCIDENT

Depending on the magnitude of our suffering or the obstacles in our way, time seemed to either stand still or rush uncomfortably by. We had made it to the spring of 1942, whose bright days and long, drawn-out evenings brought some relief to the general wretchedness caused by the cold and darkness. As usual, every time our lives seemed to be getting calmer, an unexpected event shook Prague. On May 27, Reinhard Heydrich was the target of an attack while in his car. Heydrich was one of the most important members of the SS, an official favored by Hitler and Himmler. From 1939, he was chief of the Reich Main Security Office, RSHA and from 1941, the deputy *Reichsprotektor* of Bohemia and Moravia. The attack took place while he was making the daily trip from his home in Hradčany to his headquarters. He was in a green Mercedes Benz with an open roof, displaying his customary confidence in the powers of his own arrogant, boundless and supreme authority over the resistance and his successful "pacification" of the population.

Historical records state that Heydrich managed to get out of the car, pull out his gun and shoot at his attacker before collapsing to the ground. However, his attacker was in fact not a single person but a group of Czech agents trained in England. History also says that Heydrich was seriously wounded and that Himmler immediately sent his personal doctors to Prague to save his great aide, but fragments of the car upholstery, small steel shards and fibers from his own uniform were already lodged in his spleen and caused a massive infection – a type of septicemia – that the doctors were unable to control. Finally, on Thursday, June 4, Reinhard Heydrich died. Other versions – unofficial but credible – hold that he died during the attack and that the shock wave of the grenade caused his head to explode and sprayed his brains all over the car.

These were possibly the worst moments for the country. The news, which spread like wildfire inside and outside Czechoslovakia, shook the world because of the potential consequences of the death of this feared leader. At the local level, the consequences of the attack were disastrous. Right away, the Reich adopted rigorous measures to keep the situation under control and capture the attackers. Loudspeakers were activated across the city to communicate guidelines, warnings and threats of retaliation. If anyone was suspected of approving of the attack, they were executed on the spot, and if anyone at any time and for whichever motive was found to have links with the free patriots behind the attack – who were surely hiding nearby – and failed to inform the authorities of the fact, they were also shot. If they did inform the authorities, their fate would be no better as they would be considered accomplices and killed anyway.

In the meantime, the Gestapo and the SS were arresting and killing Czech agents, members of the resistance and anyone suspected of ties to the attack against Heydrich. The number of dead reached 1,000, and 3,000 Jews were deported to Theresienstadt for later extermination; meanwhile, in Berlin, 500 Jews were arrested and 152 of them were executed in retaliation for Heydrich's death.[13] The event exacerbated the cruel harshness of the Nazi regime, whose authorities orchestrated the most perverse and varied police and military actions in a clear spirit of revenge.

A few days after the attack on Heydrich and his death, my husband and I were standing on the balcony of our apartment at Lobkovické Náměstí 9, in Prague's twelfth district – an area known as Vinohrady. From this vantage point we watched in horror as around 20 handcuffed men were pushed against a wall by the Nazi police. The Gestapo then mowed them down with wave upon wave of machine gun fire, as if to make sure that no victim could possibly be left alive, and the men began to drop dead in pools of blood and amid screams of despair. This scene was repeated several times and in between executions the bodies were loaded onto army vehicles that had previously unloaded another group of condemned men who would also soon be dead and removed from there. After around two hours, during which nearly 150 men were despicably murdered in this way, the slaughter came to an end and a chilling silence replaced the thunder of gunfire, the command voices and the victims' cries.

No comments are necessary save for this brief synthesis of our reactions: horror, indignation, disgust, sadness, nausea, vomiting, fainting and exclamations such as "Let's shut the windows!" "No, don't scream, cry in silence!" "Remember, we haven't seen a thing," "We have to get out of here as soon as possible," and "Dogs!"…. And then, as usual, we kept quiet, tried to pull ourselves together and tried to forget.

It's unbelievable: Almost 60 years have gone by and every time I remember that massacre, I feel the same trembling and the same shiver that I felt then. I still haven't been able to forget. I know I never will.

13 Editorial note: These data are unconfirmed. The Nazis retaliated by destroying two villages, Lidice and Ležáky. Beginning on 10 June, all males over the age of 16 in these villages were murdered. All the women in Ležáky were also murdered. All but four of the women from Lidice were immediately deported to Ravensbrück concentration camp. At least 1,300 people were massacred after Heydrich's death.

VISITORS IN THE NIGHT

That night, at three in the morning, we woke up with a start to the sound of boots marching, fists pounding on our front door and the doorbell ringing insistently. "Open up! Gestapo!" a voice yelled outside the door. They entered and immediately began searching and breaking everything. They even had the nerve to pick the child up out of his crib. I had just managed to make it into the bathroom to conceal a document my father had entrusted me with, placing it inside the hem of my nightgown. I was to take this document to Buenos Aires whenever I could, because I would allegedly have diplomatic protection. It was the Austrian police's reply to my husband's request from the Argentine Consulate in Prague inquiring about the motive of his arrest, back when my father was in a prison near Vienna. It was signed by Heydrich and certified that my father had been to jail simply for being an enemy of the Reich and not for fraud, theft or any other crime.

I decided to rip up the document and flush it down the toilet to avoid being asked questions about my father. I took off the nightgown and barely covered myself with it on purpose. When I came out of the bathroom, the intruders did not suspect what I had just done, and were surprised to see me emerge nearly naked. My husband added a second cause for astonishment by producing the credentials that showed he was the secretary to the Argentine consul in Prague. Although it was not an official document, it saved us on several occasions because it had his picture, was written in Spanish – a language they did not understand – and bore the seal of the Argentine Republic, a country that had so far not declared war on Germany. "Please forgive us. Why did you not tell us when we came in?" said the leader of the pack. And giving his men an order, they immediately withdrew. The nightmare had ended, but we were unable to sleep that night.

The retaliations over Heydrich's death continued. The resistance fighters who had carried out the elimination of the ruthless Nazi leader were sought out everywhere, until they were eventually betrayed by a collaborator who suggested that 20 of them might be hiding inside the deep, maze-like crypt of an old Christian temple, the Saint Cyril and Methodius Church, on Resslova and Václavská Streets, near Karlovo Náměstí. The temple's robust structure, which made it as impenetrable as a fortress, led the Reich's agents to the decision that it might be too risky to go in as they may be walking into a trap. Instead, they flooded the place, pumping water in from the nearby Vltava through large pipes installed for that purpose, and drowned them all. At that time, a former employee of my parents asked me to help those men. She was a Communist who was working with an anti-Nazi group. I gave her a few scant food items but asked her not to return because I feared the Nazis might be following her. Those were times of great danger and I had a small child to protect.

Perhaps the worst reprisals were the ones that Hitler ordered against Lidice, a small Czech village whose inhabitants were suspected by the Führer of collaborating with Heydrich's killers. His order, which was carried out on June 10, 1942, was to execute the 172 males over 16 years of age who lived in the village, while the women and children were deported to a concentration camp at Ravensbrück, where most died. Ninety children from Lidice were sent to the camp at Gneisenau,[14] while those who looked German ended up in Nazi orphanages.

Lidice was destroyed by explosives one house at a time and the rubble was then removed, leaving no trace of the village. Subsequently, earth was scattered over the leveled ground and wheat and other cereals planted to cover up the entire area where the town had once stood. *Delenda Lidice est.*[15] Lidice was even wiped from the maps, as if to deny its historical existence altogether. But it was precisely because of this that Lidice went definitively down in history, that unappealable judgment that is second only to God's.

Heydrich was dead, but the extermination machine that he had set in motion continued to mow down innocent lives until the end of the war, managed and operated by his successor Kaltenbrunner with the support of the SS, a few Nazi bureaucrats, industrialists, scientists and individuals from occupied countries. His so-called "Final Solution" led to the death in extermination camps of Jews, Roma, homosexuals, clergymen and war prisoners. Nazism's absolute power spread death and sorrow wherever it went, and made its men feel like gods.

14 Editorial note: This refers to a former textile factory in Gneisenau Street in Łódź. Eighty-one children from Lidice were killed in gas vans at the Chełmno extermination camp.

15 Lidice was wiped out.

AN INVITATION TO DIE

We had started to receive Gestapo summonses addressed to my son, who was little more than two months old at the time. Each citation indicated the time – usually seven or eight in the morning – and the place – always a Gestapo or SS headquarters – where he should show up. Those who showed up after receiving a summons were taken to a large stadium where the final selection was made. With a slight motion of his head or index finger, an official standing in front of a long line of people decided if the detainees were to go left or right. Then, following the same method, other officials broke the groups down into smaller units and sent them to concentration camps, forced labor, gas chambers or immediate death. Each summons was an invitation to death.

We knew positively what would happen to us if we meekly showed up with our child, but we had no way of fighting against these summonses other than indifference. We simply had to ignore them. By the time we had received several of them, my husband and I had come to the agreement that we would remain indifferent until they sent someone to get us. If and when that happened, we would jump from the balcony with the child to find immediate death. But they never came for us. We were among the last Jews remaining in Prague, and surely the only ones with permission to leave the country, thanks to our Argentine passports "without citizenship."

One day, we received a summons from the Czech police, which was not exactly the Gestapo. They took away our Argentine passports and gave us other "non-German" ones – we never knew the reason for this description. These were legal German documents, but they were lacking the "J" used to identify Jews. The passports we received, in fact, represented a new type of discriminatory policy, because they added the name Sarah to every Jewish woman's name, and the name Israel to that of every Jewish man. Thus, my passport showed my name as Edith Ilse Sarah Hahn de Kaufmann, my husband was Adalbert Israel Kaufmann and our son was Carlos Israel Kaufmann. We knew that those documents were passports to hell. We had been clearly identified as Jews. A simple "J" could be concealed or blurred or go unnoticed, but names spoke for themselves! We could not use these passports to try to leave the country. We were caught in a deeper trap than ever before, at a time

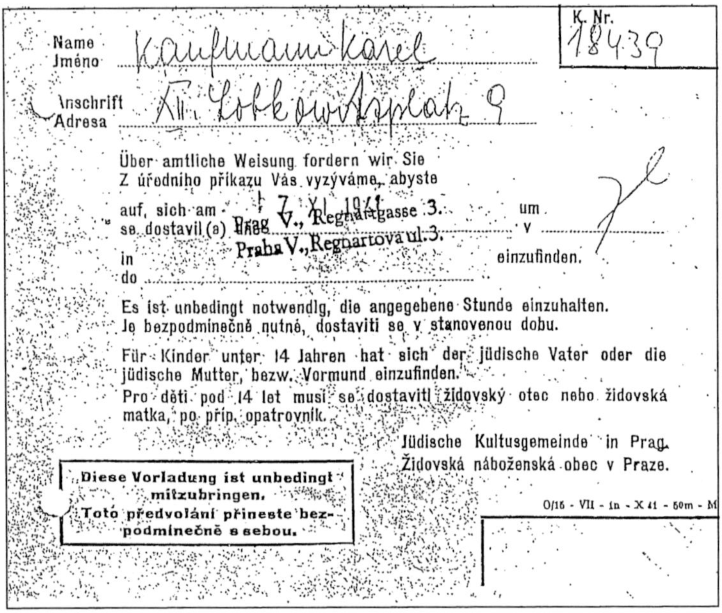

K. Nr. 18439

Name / Jméno: Kaufmann Karel

Inschrift / Adresa: XII. Lobkowitzplatz 9

Über amtliche Weisung fordern wir Sie
Z úředního příkazu Vás vyzýváme, abyste
auf, sich am 7. XI. 1941 um 7h
se dostavil(e) dne Prag V., Regnartgasse 3. v
in Praha V., Regnartova ul. 3. einzufinden.
do

Es ist unbedingt notwendig, die angegebene Stunde einzuhalten.
Je bezpodmínečně nutné, dostaviti se v stanovenou dobu.

Für Kinder unter 14 Jahren hat sich der jüdische Vater oder die jüdische Mutter, bezw. Vormund einzufinden.
Pro děti pod 14 let musí se dostaviti židovský otec nebo židovská matka, po příp. opatrovník.

Jüdische Kultusgemeinde in Prag.
Židovská náboženská obec v Praze.

Diese Vorladung ist unbedingt mitzubringen.
Toto předvolání přineste bezpodmínečně s sebou.

O/16 - VII - in - X 41 - 50m - M

Reference number: 18439

Name: Kaufmann, Karel
Address: XII Lobkowitzplatz 9

By official order, you are requested to show up on

November 7, 1941 at seven in the morning
at Prague V, Regnartova Str. 3.

It is absolutely necessary to respect the indicated time.

Children under 14 years of age must be accompanied by their Jewish father or mother, or by a tutor.

Prague Jewish Community

This summons must be shown upon arrival.

A summons addressed to Carlos Kaufmann (who was two months old at the time) for attendance at the Prague Jewish Community, which was under Nazi control.

when we could no longer stand the pressure of the surrounding danger. It was just another one of the ways in which war liked to taunt us.

WORSE THINGS WERE HAPPENING

I received a letter from my Grandmother Mathilde, who was living with my Aunt Alicia in Olmütz, the beautiful Moravian town that had meant so much to me. We had known for some time that Aunt Alicia had had to give up her luxurious apartment on Nazi orders and had moved to a modest place that she shared with Willy Groak's family – the young man I danced with at the *Purim* celebration and who later became my fiancé. Willy's family had also been evicted from their comfortable home in Olmütz, which, just like my aunt's, had been immediately occupied by the family of a Nazi bigwig, who not only enjoyed its spacious rooms but also its rich furniture and luxurious ornaments.

Both Aunt Alicia and Willy Groak's family had also had to turn over their valuables to the invaders, and were living on very little money. Aunt Alicia was getting weaker all the time. Her fragility could not stand the adversity, the humiliation, the hardship and the fear. She positively knew that she and her mother were already sentenced to death. In her letter, my Grandmother Mathilde said that in two weeks they would in all likelihood be taken to a concentration camp, and hinted that she feared they would be killed in the gas chambers. She asked me to try to get to Olmütz so we could see each other one last time. It was a simple letter. It was written in plain, realistic terms that held no sign of hope. It also evidenced a complete and incredible resignation, and showed such sweetness for me that it was hard to read it without falling into despair. I cried bitter tears that could not save my grandmother or aunt. Crying over other people's tragedies does not solve their problems; it just makes the person who is crying feel better. And sometimes, not even that.

I told my husband that I wanted to go to Olmütz, and he agreed to come with me. Our son would be cared for by Berta, my childhood governess, who was still helping my son and me. I left enough breast milk for several feedings in the ice box, because, as I explained earlier, it was not possible to buy milk for Jewish children and it would have been careless to expose Carlos, who was so little, to such a trip. It is probably unnecessary to say that the reunion with my grandmother and aunt was heartbreaking. My grandmother was 66 and a beautiful lady. She looked like a queen. My aunt, who had just turned 45, still had some beauty left despite her weak state and extreme bitterness. In spite of the emotion of the moment and the painful situation ahead of them, they both maintained an attitude of dignity and resigned fortitude at all times. We only broke down into choked sobs and tears of despair later, when the time came to say goodbye…forever.

SURROUNDED BY DEATH

We returned to Prague that same night, feeling devastated. We also knew that Willy Groak, who was now married, had been sent with his wife to Theresienstadt, and from there to an extermination camp. Years later, after the war, we learned that only he had returned. We suddenly felt that death was getting closer and closer, stalking us, surrounding us.

During the trip home, feeling in shock but trying not to show it so as not to attract suspicious looks, we quietly told each other that we had to get out of Europe as soon as possible. Aunt Alicia and my Grandmother Mathilde, knowing that our savings had been depleted after paying to get my parents out of Europe, gave us some of their own remaining money and a few things to sell or trade for food or anything else we might need. They knew their time was up, while ours was about to begin. We were in need of some luck, and the items they had given us would certainly help in the days prior to our departure. Anyway, if we had not taken these goods, the Nazis would have confiscated them. However, the few Reichsmark they had given us were useless as they could only be used in Germany or its occupied territories and were not accepted as foreign currency.

When we arrived home, Carlos was sleeping peacefully in his crib, his little arms spread on either side of his head, his hands slightly curled into soft fists and his cheeks warm and rosy. He was the very image of serenity and I thanked the Lord at that moment. Berta was sitting by his side, rocking the cradle rhythmically with her foot. After going through so much pain in Olmütz, seeing that wonderful scene and finding my son safe and sound and pampered moved me deeply. I took him out of his crib and held him against my breast for a long time, feeling love wash over me. His mere presence made me forget all my sadness and sorrow. He represented complete and utter joy.

We spent the following days preparing for the trip, carefully selecting what we would take with us, how we would carry it and what to leave behind, painful though it was. Our luggage had to be discreet and we had to travel light. We had to carry the child, who was one year and three months old, and already weighed 10-12 kilos. We also had two shabby-looking suitcases – the only ones we could buy – which were small but packed with clothes and also heavy. To that we had to add a trunk, which I still keep, for our bedclothes and the baby carriage. Berta said she would take care of any items that we wanted to hold on to and which she could slowly take over to her place without raising any suspicion.

When everything was finally organized, we sold some of the things we were leaving behind to the trade attaché at the consulate. They were the items we had bought with the money from Marko Heller's legacy to furnish our apartment on Lobcovické Náměstí: some furniture, a couple of rugs, a few paintings and some ornaments, which together made for a meager sum of money, but one which would be useful for the trip. Making use of the diplomatic protection we were privileged to have, we agreed that in order to avoid the risk of having the money confiscated at the border, it would be wired to us through the Bank of Bilbao when we arrived in Spain.

MOVING LETTERS

In the middle of these preparations, we received another letter from my Grandmother Mathilde in Olmütz, which she had written on July 4, the day before being deported with Aunt Alicia to Theresienstadt. This is what my grandmother wrote:

> *Olmütz, July 4, 1942*
>
> *My three beloved children,*
> *Thank you so much for the Serdomit* [a tranquilizer], *which unfortunately I can no longer find here, and thank you very, very much for your lovely letter of July 2. May God allow us to see each other again in good health. But I do not think so. I cannot think and do not wish to. Keep my paintings; I don't know whether I sent them to you already.*

My Ilse, there was nothing in this world I loved more than you, my little one. My only fervent prayer is always for my children's well-being and for a happy reunion. Yes, Alicia was always getting mad at my accent, but she always fulfilled her duties as a daughter and took perfect care of everything all by herself, for the both of us.

Help her on the eve of our goodbyes; I have to say that she was always there for me and God should reward her. I pray that the two of us will not be separated. This is the last time I will be in a bed. My little Ilse, be brave and pray to God because you were always the best child and always fulfilled your duties towards us, my love. God bless you and protect you for all eternity. Amen.

I will write again tomorrow. Your loving grandmother and great-grandmother.

Rosa's address [one of her sisters] *is 11 Kraftgasse 6 Albersheim AA 0674. Please do not forget this number. Alicia will write her own letter. Right now she is very distressed because of the weight* [of the bag she will carry when she is deported].

We also received a letter from Aunt Alicia. It does not bear a date or place name, but she must have written it that same day in Olmütz. Her words show her great love for us, but also the depth of her well-justified dejection.

My darling little Ilse and dear Bela,
Thank you very much for those last lines you wrote. They afforded some consolation to me in the midst of my enormous misfortune. I am deathly tired and spent. It is one in the morning and I am in bed. My last time in a bed, where I always rested so peacefully. A stomach and intestinal flu; too weak to breathe, and tomorrow the fourth journey from Olmütz in the harshest conditions because it is a journey of punishment. Ten kilos of provisions but the bag itself already weighs ten kilos, so I will have to leave the provisions behind. We will go like Putzi at the villa [their little dog at Veilchen Villa in Vöslau]. *There are just a few hours left until the end. I think of you and hope that you will have happy lives. I am more than grateful for your kindness. Did Tomy* [Ambassador Carlos Tomás Brunel] *receive the 30 crowns from Rosi? Ask him. I don't know why God abandoned me like this and why I have to suffer so much. I am so*

tired. I wish all the best for you. Stay in good health and do not forget your poor unfortunate

Alicia.

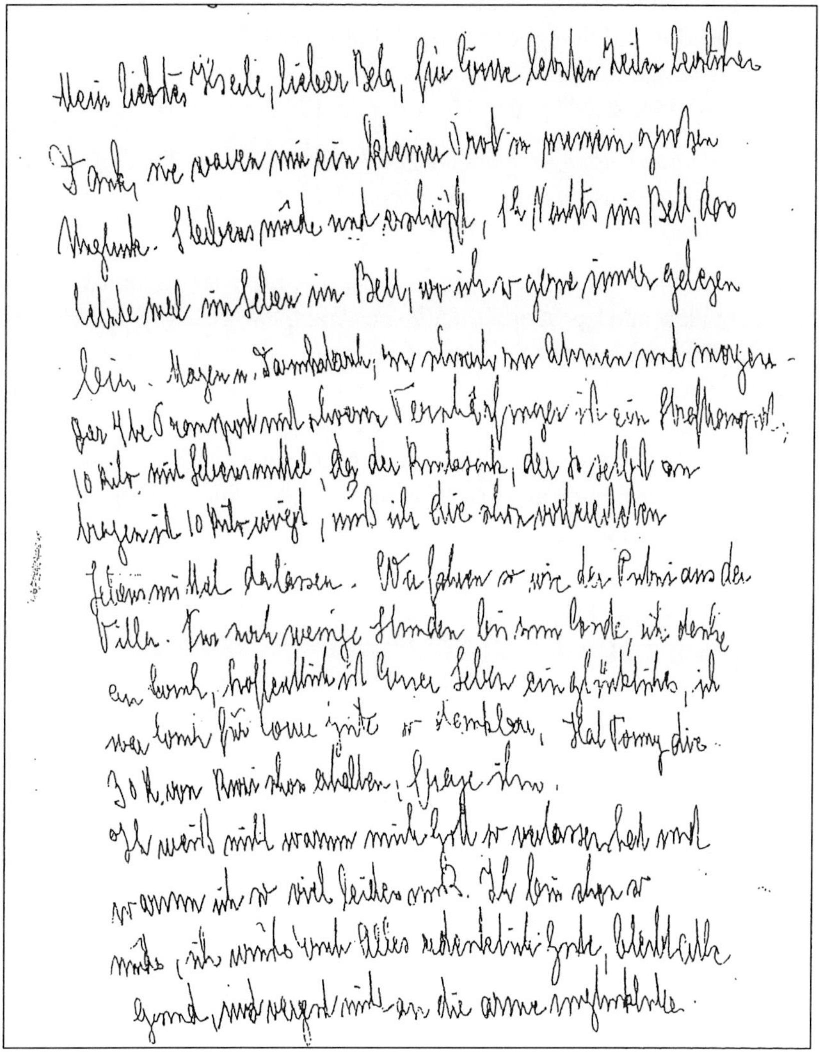

The last letter written and mailed by Alicia Heller (Aunt Alicia) before being deported to Theresienstadt.

In the days before the trip, I received a new letter, this time from Theresienstadt, which I also keep as a treasure. It is a painful memento of my Grandmother Mathilde. With a trembling hand, she wrote her last goodbyes on a small piece of paper. She knew that death was awaiting her at a concentration camp and she said farewell with such sweet words of affection that I choked on my own tears as I read it and thought I would die of sorrow. It was truly tremendous. Aunt Alicia would follow in her footsteps.

My grandmother's letter, whose original I have also preserved, says:

> *My dears, I hope you are in good health. We are healthy as well. I will write again as soon as I can. One thousand kisses. Your loving grandmother.*

On the back, there is the following address: Frau Ilse Kaufmann Prag XII 9 Lobkowitz Platz and a post office stamp bearing the words "Prag-25, Praha 25" 31.VII.42. We later learned that when they were deported to Auschwitz, these two women who had once been so wealthy took nothing more with them than a thin mattress rolled up under their arms and a small bag with a few clothes, some personal effects and hardly any food. Later, when the war ended, my husband wrote to the Prague authorities in my mother's name asking about them. The reply confirmed what we had feared: Neither one of them had returned from Auschwitz. The official note says:

> *Mrs. Karoline Hahn*
> *Malabia 2743,*
> *Buenos Aires*
> *Argentina*
>
> *We would like to inform you that Mathilde Goldschmidt, born on 23.2.1876, and Alicia Heller, born on 20.6.1897, both living in Olmütz at the last known date, were both deported to Theresienstadt for racial motives on 8.7.1942 on Transportation No. AAo-674/675. Mathilde Goldschmidt was deported from Theresienstadt to Auschwitz on 15.12.1943 and did not return. Alicia Heller was deported from Theresienstadt to an unknown destination on 28.7.1942 and did not return.*
> *From 1.9.1941 both had to wear the Jewish star.*
>
> *Jewish Community Council of the Czech Socialist Republic*
> *Ing. Fr. Fuchs O. Heitlinger*

No doubt, when my grandmother wrote from Olmütz on July 4 giving me Rosa's address and asking me not to forget the number, she was telling me the number of the transportation that would take them to Theresienstadt – Transportation No. AAo-674. It was the note from the Jewish Community Council that alerted us to the coincidence regarding these two numbers.

OUR JOURNEY TOWARDS LIFE

On Saturday, December 12, 1942, at eight o'clock on a dark and snowy morning that turned into a windy, freezing, overcast day, we placed little Carlos inside a fur-lined carry cot to protect him from the harsh winter cold, grabbed our scant luggage, turned off the lights in our apartment, and, as though the curtain was going down on this period of our lives, we shut the door and walked away.

It is easy now, almost 60 years later, to say that we just closed the door and walked away. After receiving so many summonses requesting that Carlos report to the authorities, no doubt to be taken to the gas chambers; saying goodbye forever to my grandmother and aunt; receiving their letters, written the day before being deported to Theresienstadt; and with the memory of the massacre of Czech men in front of our house still fresh in my mind; as well as the constant fear that had hounded me for months, turning off the lights, closing the door and walking away was not a spur-of-the-moment decision. It was a new risk that we were taking, but we took it willingly, spurred on by the desire to get away from that long, interminable nightmare. So, we turned off the lights, shut the door and walked away. It was that simple. It was that thrilling.

Berta was with us. She was to come with us as far as Dresden, our first stop in Germany. From there, she would make her way home to the Sudetenland, while we would continue to Paris. Ambassador Brunel helped us one last time by driving us to the train station. Once there, he presented us with a suitcase containing food for the trip: boiled ham, cheese, bread, condensed milk for the child – quite a luxury in the middle of a war – and a bottle of cognac from Greece, a country with which he had diplomatic ties. Hours later, this bottle would save our lives.

When we arrived, the station was very crowded, because many soldiers were traveling home on their holiday leave. The Nazi government was withholding the truth about the situation at the front, which was not good, and was trying to keep the soldiers and their families happy by allowing them to spend Christmas together. The general confusion at the station was good for us, since it allowed us to go by unnoticed. When the time came to say goodbye, Ambassador Carlos Brunel, a man who loved Argentina very much, became slightly nostalgic and visibly emotional as he told us, "You are traveling to paradise. Argentina is the most beautiful country in existence. The skies are blue there and the sun and the stars shine with a stronger light in that clear open sky." My husband translated his words for me and I believe I remember them correctly. I would say that the love for Argentina that I still profess began to take shape in my heart at that time.

The train departed 20 minutes late – an unusual occurrence – and then we began our journey towards a new life. That was our destination. I was leaving behind a happy childhood, the misfortunes of war, all kinds of deprivations, constant moves, beautiful Prague, the Moldau River, the prisons where my father had been unfairly jailed, and the feeling of fear. I was taking thousands of memories with me, along with a small suitcase, a husband obtained in the strangest possible manner – and who was already a great companion to me – and the fruit of our marriage, our son Carlos, who made us feel so close and whom we loved so dearly.

It was almost mid-morning. The sky was gray and there were heavy storm clouds in the sky, but we were calm and beginning to feel happy. I could almost see the sun at the end of the road, and meanwhile Carlos was being lulled into sleep by the warmth of the carry cot.

THE TRAIN RIDE

After crossing the Czech-German border, our train skirted around Theresienstadt, the small Czech town in northwestern Bohemia where, between 1941 and 1945, the Nazis operated a ghetto for Jews from central and western Europe who were gradually deported to extermination camps.

Despite the morning mist, we were able to make out a great many people working in the rain and standing in the snow, and even managed to spy the profile of the fateful camp that we were escaping from. I did not want to think about it, but my heart screamed out that our loved ones – those who were not lucky enough to get away – were there, or had been there, or would soon be there, enduring the pain of arrogance, the menacing barks of the Doberman dogs, the constant corrosive humiliation of bosses and subordinates, and the most atrocious, unjustifiable and senseless physical suffering. From the train window, through glass that was frosted on the outside and misty on the inside, I gazed sadly at this scene in a last goodbye that was soon clouded by tears. Theresienstadt and its dramatic story was left behind, but those of us who saw it with our own eyes still carry the memory within us, like a suppressed sob.

We arrived in Dresden approximately 20 minutes late, at around five in the afternoon. When we got off the train, we asked which platform the Paris-bound train was departing from, but were alarmed to learn that it had already left. Our delay out of Prague had thrown us off schedule. It was getting dark and it was very cold. Since there was still a regulation in force prohibiting Jews from staying in hotels, we feared for our safety. Where would we go? Where could we find shelter from the wind and the rain? All our hard work of the previous day – the packing, the decision-making and the planning in the middle of so much tension – had left us feeling exhausted. Besides, we were undernourished and, as I said, it was very cold.

We stored part of our belongings inside a locker and then my husband walked to a hotel across from the train station. He spoke to the concierge, explaining that we needed a room for the night, that we had enough money to pay in advance, but warning him that we were Jewish so as not to put him in a difficult situation. The man was very cordial and sympathetic. He told my husband that he was 75 years old and did not care what religion we professed, adding that he had had many Jewish clients in the past who had been very courteous and generous. He also said that he had been a happy man until the Nazis rose to power, but that the Reich's policies had taken away his peace of mind and filled him with sadness.

We were given a very large and comfortable suite, with good heating and hot water, and were told that food could be brought to the room. However, that was not a problem for us since we had Ambassador Brunel's suitcase full of food. We placed Carlos in the middle of the bed, which was large and made up with impeccable bed linen, and suddenly felt so tired that we each lay down on either side of the child without even taking our clothes off – just our shoes. Berta, to whom we had given our remaining Reichsmarks after paying for the hotel so she could use them in German territory – where they were worth something – lay down on a sofa in the entrance and we all fell into a deep slumber. We woke up 20 hours later. Berta had left without waking us up, very likely to let us get some rest but perhaps also to avoid a painful goodbye.

Everything was happening fast now. It was almost time to board the train that would take us to Paris. We barely had time to clean up a bit, prepare a bottle for Carlos with hot water provided by the hotel, change his diaper and get back to the station in time to board the train. It was unbearably cold, but we were feeling better.

PARIS-BOUND

It was past noon on Sunday, December 13, 1942, when we left for Paris. At the precise moment when the train was pulling out of the station, a young couple climbed on and walked into our compartment. They were both tall, slim, blond and visibly agitated. She was wearing elegant clothes and he wore a Nazi uniform with badges indicating that he was a high-ranking official. When he strode in, he gave the Nazi salute and said in a clear, firm voice: "*Heil*, Hitler!" To which we replied with a simple "good day" and a courteous head gesture that was meant to disguise our disagreement with the Führer's god-like condition implicit in this salute. Fortunately, the official did not seem displeased at our attitude, and while we tried not to show how terrified we were, the two settled into their seats and it soon became obvious from their behavior that they were in love. Soon after, when a conversation of sorts began between us, they told us they were just married and on their way to Paris for their honeymoon.

My husband and I were now in a truly difficult position, but there was nothing we could do. We could not speak to each other, not even in Czech, because they might understand that language. We could not exchange meaningful looks or talk in a low voice or use coded language. We could not write messages to each other because that would be clumsy and suspicious. The only thing we could do was to disguise our fear as best we could. Carlos and his babyish antics made it easier to deal with a situation that was tricky, dangerous and, frankly, also ridiculous; if either one of us had ever envisioned such a possibility, the other would have called it delirious thinking. Was this not the most absurd thing that could happen to us on our flight from the Nazi regime? It was truly one of life's ironies.

And then, just half an hour into the trip, something unexpected happened that solved our problem. The Nazi official began acting like he was in pain. He was developing a toothache that soon intensified to the point of making him seem a completely changed person; his face contorted and turned pale as a sheet. This man who had delivered his "*Heil*, Hitler!" so vigorously was now a trembling, whimpering human being who was doubled over in pain. This new image of him was, truth be told, very different from the manly, dashing figure he had cut when he strode into our compartment – very likely the figure that his new wife had fallen in love with and admired. Neither they, nor we, had any painkillers to soothe the Nazi official's suffering. We were now concerned about the change of mood inside the microcosm of our train compartment. I could see the concern in my husband's eyes and he could probably see it in mine. The child's antics were beginning to bother the SS official and his wife looked very nervous. An unpleasant, trying trip stretched ahead of us.

Then I noticed Ambassador Brunel's suitcase. Inside, I knew, was a bottle of Greek cognac. We explained to the official that we had a bottle of cognac that was a parting gift from the ambassador of Argentina and took this opportunity to inform him that the ambassador himself had driven us to the station in his car, all of which put us in an advantageous position in the eyes of the SS official. This introduction allowed us to offer him the cognac as a possible painkiller and also provided a chance for my husband to introduce himself as a member of that embassy and show the official his embassy card – the one he always carried and which had saved our lives once already, when that nasty official at Gestapo headquarters in Prague had made me stand for hours while he interrogated me about my father and Bestiak the engineer. Even though it was not an official document, it had helped us escape from the Nazis' clutches once and might be useful again.

The SS official accepted a bit of cognac and soon began talking about Argentina, telling us that Germany would win the war, then invade England, then go to Argentina, which was an ally because it was a country that had not declared war on Germany.[16] He asked us for our address in Buenos Aires and we told him that we still did not have a fixed domicile but that the embassy's chancellery there would give him our contact information. Suddenly, there were voices outside and the door of our compartment flew open. Three Gestapo men on a routine check were asking all passengers for their identification papers. We felt ourselves sinking. Our passports, which had us down as Sarah and Israel, could get us thrown off the train at the very next stop and then God only knows what would become of us. The only thing that could save us now was the Argentine Embassy credential, even if it was not official.

Fortunately, no sooner had they extended their arms and exclaimed "*Heil*, Hitler!" than our uniformed traveling companion jumped to his feet to return the standard salute, while he proudly exhibited his credentials attesting that he was a member of the Führer's closest secretarial staff. They all exchanged respectful and self-complacent remarks and when the guards turned to us to ask for our papers, the SS official – perhaps because of the cognac we had offered him, or because he felt sympathy towards us because of our ties to Argentina, or perhaps because God chose to send us a guardian angel – dissuaded them. "That won't be necessary. They are my friends," said the official. And all three men followed his orders, raising their arms in the air, clicking their heels and turning before walking away. We had long since learned to conceal our inner fears, so we kept outwardly calm during this entire exchange, and although I never knew how I found the strength to do so, I immediately offered the suffering official more cognac, handing him the bottle so he could pour himself the occasional dose of painkiller.

Things had quieted down again. The SS official slowly drank the cognac. He drank and drank and drank, seeking solace from the pain. He was getting drunk without realizing it, until he finally became completely intoxicated. He began snoring most disagreeably; he was sweating, and his features were shiny and flushed from the effects of the alcohol and the heat washing over his body. No doubt as a subconscious reaction against such an unromantic scene, especially during their honeymoon, his new wife curled up on her seat, shut her eyes and let the rhythmic sound of the train lull her to sleep as well. Soon, she began to relax and finally she fell into a deep slumber that took her far away from the saddening sight of her hero snoring away with his mouth hanging open and his cheeks sagging like bags on either side of his chin.

16 Argentina was at that time a neutral country.

IN THE MIDDLE OF THE FIELDS, THE NIGHT AND THE SILENCE

Several hours went by and we were already hundreds of kilometers from the horror we had left behind. The train sometimes stopped in the middle of a snowy field in the dead of night and the silence then was awesome. Other times, we stopped at train stations for longer than we thought was normal. Each time the pace changed, our hearts started beating faster and we quietly went into alert mode. The main thing for us was to keep advancing further and further away from hell and towards Spain.

Our traveling companions were both in a deep sleep and we did not know whether that was good or bad for us. The less we talked to them, the fewer the chances of being asked risky questions, but we could not ignore the fact that the sympathy the SS official felt for us had already borne fruit once, when he described us as "his friends" to the guards. My husband and I decided to take turns sleeping, despite the fact that we were both equally exhausted. It was the only way of taking care of Carlos and keeping an eye out for anything unusual that might happen. It was just one more interminable night of the many we experienced during those years.

At one point the train stopped, we heard voices outside and someone said that there was an air raid going on near our next destination. We could hear loud explosions and the sound of planes in the distance that confirmed what we had overheard. The sound of cannons and machine gun fire put the finishing touches on this war concert that our companions slept right through. The train then came to a complete stop and all was still — extremely still — the way a feline is still when it senses danger. The lights were turned out and a tense, anguished silence took hold of the darkness inside the train. Fortunately, Carlos slept and so did the couple.

This situation continued for what seemed like an eternity. Later, when the explosions ended, a spine-tingling silence fell over everything, and without blowing the whistle, like a crouching cat whose fur stops standing on end and whose muscles relax once again, the train began moving — slowly, as though fearfully or cautiously — while the wheels screeched quietly but painfully over the rails. It was a moment of paralyzing suspense during which we held our breath and prayed in silence. Later, the train gradually began picking up speed again and our own distress began subsiding until we finally heard the regular, comforting rhythm of the train returning to its regular speed. We remained poker-faced on the outside while we collapsed on the inside.

PARIS

We arrived in Paris on Monday, December 14, very early in the morning. It was still dark and the damp, penetrating cold felt even more intense because we were so tired and had not had anything warm to eat or drink for many hours. The SS official and his wife were already awake and ready to get off the train. They said goodbye kindly, thanked us for the cognac and left. A few seconds later, my husband found a wallet on the floor of the train compartment containing money and documents, which the official had obviously dropped. Without a moment's hesitation, he jumped off the train and ran across the platform to return what was rightfully theirs. Although I did not disapprove, privately I could not help thinking about that episode in Prague when I had bought two kilos of rice with a voucher from Ambassador Brunel, who gave it to us precisely because he could not obtain rice with it. And I remembered how, when my husband saw the "white gold" that Frau Zipfelhauben had sold me, he decided that any rice obtained with the ambassador's voucher belonged to the ambassador. A few minutes later, the SS official returned with a nurse in a spotless NSV[17] uniform, who was carrying a tray with hot coffee for us and milk, white bread and butter for Carlos. It was a tasty breakfast – the likes of which we had not enjoyed for a long time – and it was very good for the child, who quickly ate everything on his plate.

We thanked the SS official for this kindness and he again expressed gratitude for the bottle of cognac and for returning his wallet. After he and the nurse had left, my husband and I concluded that God was, without a doubt, watching over us.

17 Nationalsozialistische Volkswohlfahrt (National Socialist People's Welfare) – a social welfare organization during the Third Reich.

HEADED FOR SPAIN

To continue on our journey to Spain we had to take another train that was leaving Paris around noon. This time we would be traveling third class, rather than first, and this turned out to be a trying trip because the compartment was very uncomfortable and had no heating. For six anxiety-ridden hours the train took us across France, a country that was occupied by the Nazis, which meant that any setback would cause us to be sent straight to Poland and the gas chambers. The train was full and we managed to only get one seat, so we took turns resting and holding the child in our lap.

On the way from Paris to Hendaye there was a new Gestapo document check. When they saw our passports with the names Sarah and Israel on them, they asked how it was possible for Jews to be traveling on that train bound for Spain and threatened to make us get off. They only calmed down when my husband showed them the note from the Argentine Foreign Affairs Ministry and a document granting permission to leave any territories ruled by the Reich, issued by the German Foreign Affairs Ministry and stamped in Berlin. Both documents stated that Adalbert Kaufmann, his wife Edith Ilse Kaufmann and their child Carlos Kaufmann were authorized to leave Germany and the German-occupied territories.

At around eight in the evening, we arrived in Hendaye, on the border with Spain. If we managed to cross the border into Irún, we would be safe. The closer we got to our goal, the more nervous we became that any misstep, any imprudence or any misfortune might ruin our plans at the last minute. The train slowed down as it approached Hendaye. We grabbed our things, wrapped Carlos in blankets and stepped out onto a nearly empty platform that was dark and snowy. We were still on French territory under German occupation and we still had one more Nazi checkpoint to go through. Men and women were separated and a humiliating body search began during which we not only had to take off all our clothes, despite the intense cold, but the women even had their genitals checked. However, they did not touch Carlos, who slept peacefully in his carry cot. We weren't hiding anything between the baby's sheets, but it would have been a good place to do so had we had anything worth hiding. Our entire capital was five dollars and I was wearing an extremely fine gold chain around my neck that was almost invisible, with a tiny *mezuzah* hanging from it that my father had given me for protection, and which I had promised to wear at all times. When the woman who was checking me made me face her, I slipped the *mezuzah* around to the back of my neck, then to the front when I had my back to her. She either did not notice what I was doing or decided to ignore it.

FIRST STAGE IN SPAIN: IRÚN

We made it through the Nazi checkpoint at Hendaye without trouble and got back on the train, which took us across the border and into Spanish territory. A new life full of hope and expectations was opening up in front of us. We had managed to escape danger and the Nazi horror. We could consider ourselves very lucky indeed, even if great difficulties still lay ahead. We were young and fear was already starting to become little more than a memory.

As we got near our first Spanish destination, the train started to slow down. I was feeling elated at having escaped the Reich's oppression and was confident that all our suffering would now be transformed into happiness, all our anguish into hope and all our tears into crystal-clear drops of refreshing dew. With a sound that seemed like a snort, the train came to a halt and we saw a sign in front of us with the name of the town written on it. But because of the poor lighting and the smoke coming out of the smokestack, which got mixed with the morning fog, we were unable to read the letters. Only when the heavy engine's last bellow blew the smoke aside did we read what the sign said: We had arrived in Irún. There was no doubt about it. We were in Spain and that meant we were finally free.

We felt exhausted, undernourished and dehydrated. It was cold and Carlos was uncomfortable. We needed to change his diaper, feed him and put him in a warm bed, so we had to find a place to spend the night that was not too far from the station, since even the weight of our scant luggage was too much for us to bear right then. Also, we had no money. We noticed a humble-looking hotel near the station, just an inn, really. We went in and they gave us a small room that contained a narrow bed with a white iron frame, a sorry-looking bedside table and an unstable chair. I changed Carlos, fed him and put him to bed warm and calm. I thanked the Lord. We stretched out on the bed as best we could, one on either side of the child, and just like we did in Dresden, we fell into an exhausted sleep in our clothes and slept right through to the next day.

In the morning, my husband went to the local branch of the Bank of Bilbao to see if the Argentine Embassy's commercial attaché in Prague had wired the money he had agreed to pay us when we sold him the furniture and other items in our apartment. We had made these arrangements so that the cash would not be confiscated during our trip. However, the money had not arrived. The attaché, Thomas Manson, was married to a Nazi woman and this couple had moved into the apartment on the ground floor of Lobkovickè Náměstí 9 – the same building where we had lived – as soon as the janitor's family had been deported to Theresienstadt because they – and especially his wife – had been helping Jews. The janitor's wife never returned from the concentration camp, but her husband did, and later, under the Communist regime, he held a high-ranking post. For years, he and my husband kept up a sporadic correspondence.

When my husband realized he was faced with the need to pay the hotel bill, he handed his watch to the bank clerk, who gave him around 150 pesetas for it. In addition to paying the hotel bill, that money allowed us to buy third-class tickets to Bilbao, where we would take a ship to Argentina. I never found out whether my husband pawned the watch or if it had been a simple barter. He also managed to trade in three Johnny-brand cigarettes for two oranges, explaining that we were immigrants who had just crossed the border fleeing the Nazi regime. Carlos had never seen oranges before and he even ate the peel. It had been nearly two years since I had eaten fruit myself, but I was content with just one mouthful, because I could see how much my son needed them and I enjoyed seeing his happiness. We could not afford to buy anything else.

Later that morning, we packed our things, checked out of the hotel and crossed over to the train station to continue our journey. The train made stops at every station and suddenly, as we were pulling out of one of them, I noticed a trunk sitting on the platform that looked very much like mine. I nearly screamed out to my husband that our luggage was being left behind. It turned out that we were supposed to get off there and take a different train headed for Bilbao. However, it was too late, so we remained on the train until the next station and tried to turn back, but we had no money for the fare. We felt crushed by this setback, not knowing where we were or what to do. For the first time since war had wreaked havoc in Europe, leading to chronic food shortages, we spotted an establishment that included a bar and a fruit shop. The fruit was hanging from the door and was displayed behind the store windows, just like in pre-war Europe. We went in and asked for hot water to prepare a milk bottle for Carlos.

The people there, surprised at our untidy look – which at this point was a sign of how undeniably tired we were – began to ask us questions. We explained that we were war fugitives who had just arrived in Spain. Upon hearing this, the people at the bar decided to help us out. They gave us hot coffee and milk, *churros* [fried dough strips] and buns with jam, and their friendly attitude was very comforting to us after so many vicissitudes. We began chatting to them – my husband acting as translator – and they learned that we had lost our luggage and had no money to go and get it back.

The news quickly spread around the bar that there was a young couple with a small child who were Jewish refugees and on their way to Buenos Aires. They could hardly believe it. They were still very sensitive to these issues because of the civil war that had recently left its own painful mark on Spain, so they immediately sympathized to the point that they collected enough money for our train fare back to the station where we should have disembarked in the first place. Once there, we would have to take a train to Bilbao where we would probably find our things, since they had tags indicating that this was their final destination. Besides money for the rail fare, the locals also gave us a package containing a loaf of bread, ham, cheese, fruit and other food items. At this point, there were nearly 30 people milling around us. They all walked us to the station and when the train departed they waved goodbye – the men holding their hats and caps in the air and the women doing the same with their headscarves.

Ever since that day, I have felt endless gratitude and a special affection for Spaniards. I will never forget their warmth and kindness – expressed with typical Spanish generosity that I had never seen until then – at a time when we had experienced so much hardship and witnessed so many examples of wickedness and injustice.

SECOND STAGE IN SPAIN: BILBAO

Thanks to these people who went so far as to give us their money, once in Bilbao we were able to hire a horse-drawn carriage to take us to the Hotel Inglaterra, where we would finally get in touch with an organization called HICEM that was founded by the Jewish community in the United

States.[18] This group, which still exists, was on a mission to save Jews from Nazi persecution and provide them with the means to survive during their first moments of freedom, until they found a job that allowed them to, at least, begin to earn a living. From now on, we would be protected by this organization through its delegation in Spain and its representatives in Bilbao.

The first thing we saw when we entered the hotel lobby was a larger-than-life portrait of Hitler. We thought we would faint right there and then and were about to turn around and leave when the hotel owner showed up. Mrs. Löfler told us that she was English and that we could trust her. She also informed us that her husband was German and that there were Gestapo men watching the border between Spain and occupied France, prowling around the Pyrenees – especially at the Irún crossing – in search of fugitives to take back to Germany. These men, she said, did not watch the hotel because its owner, her husband, was a German national who paid tribute to the Führer by displaying an enormous portrait of him wearing his stiff-looking uniform and giving the Nazi salute. Furthermore, they did not suspect that the hotel had an agreement with HICEM and afforded covert protection to fugitives. We listened to her with growing alarm, as these confessions were the last thing we thought we would hear in Spain. They were also the last thing we wanted to hear, just when we thought we were safe. As if the English lady's explanations were not upsetting enough, just then a young man wearing a Hitler Youth uniform walked down the stairs, swastika and all. He was the Löflers' son.

Nothing there was making us feel relaxed. Everything seemed strange and suspicious, but we were caught in the web and had little choice: Either we stayed at the hotel, trusting our hosts yet keeping our eyes open, or we could stay out in the cold, with no money and no protection. The fear that had subsided into a memory when we crossed the French-Spanish border returned once more to toy with our weariness, our expectations and our yearning for peace and quiet. But, suddenly, everything changed again. At dinner, we saw that most of the tables in the hotel's dining room were filled with Jews, many of whom were French. We started a conversation with some of them and learned to our relief that everything Mrs. Löfler had told us was true: There was a deal

18 HICEM was established in 1927 as a partnership among three Jewish migration agencies: Hebrew Sheltering and Immigrant Aid Society (HIAS), Jewish Colonization Association (ICA) and the European Emigdirect.

between the Löflers and HICEM and there were upwards of 80 Jewish people staying there at that time. This, translated into pesetas, was a considerable source of income for the hotel, especially taking into account the fact that this figure had remained stable for a long while and would presumably remain that way for quite some time.

We also found out that many fugitives were coming in from France every day. Sometimes entire families crossed the Pyrenees on foot, making extraordinary efforts and enduring the cold, rain, wind, dark nights, hunger and complete lack of protection. They were driven on by the fear of being discovered by the Gestapo's hounds – the canines and the humans – who patrolled both sides of the border. Most of the fugitives were French Jews, but there were also Poles, Czechs and Germans. They all arrived with swollen legs, their feet covered with bruises, cuts and sores, their clothes torn by branches and stones, the women's features disfigured, the men with long beards, and all of them smelling bad. They were running away. It was something unnatural in humans – an animalistic reaction to danger, which war made necessary, indispensable, unpostponable and irreplaceable. They were running and it no longer mattered what their race or their creed was, whether they were rich or poor, wise or ignorant. What mattered, even if it seems like a paradox, was whether they had the courage to flee, to face the multiple risks the escape entailed, to overcome the paralyzing fear that made you postpone the decision, because if you did not escape at the right moment, it would be too late, far too late. Yes, it was important to be courageous and to love life very much.

We slowly began to relax and joined this group of people who had so much in common with us. Christmas Eve came around and there was a party at the hotel with dinner and dancing that lasted until the early hours of Christmas Day. The food was plentiful and tasty and Carlos, who was barely one year and three months, ate with a hearty appetite the entire time that he was there, laughing and enjoying all these good things. My husband and I also enjoyed the dinner, which we needed so badly, both physically and spiritually. The tables were tastefully set, there was a beautiful Christmas tree and the entire hotel was decorated and lit up. Seeing all of these things that had been so foreign to us in recent years was like taking a dip in a pool of joy that cleansed our spirit of impurities and unfair suffering and gave us renewed hope.

When the end of 1942 came round a week later, the hotel organized another party to celebrate Saint Sylvester and toast the coming year, which was full of hope for all the guests there. This period of revelry and merriment did us the world of good. Besides, it was all new to us, since in Vienna these celebrations – especially Christmas Eve and Christmas Day – had a much more religious meaning. When the church bells rang at midnight on December 24, all Christian families went to mass. Afterwards, when the faithful emerged from their respective churches, they all wished each other good luck while the singing inside the temples still lingered in the air, prolonging the liturgical atmosphere as everyone walked home on snowy streets filled with the smell of roasting chestnuts sold by street vendors. On December 25, homes served a traditional roast goose for Christmas lunch, which brought family members together again. *Stille Nacht* (Silent Night) was always sung at these family gatherings. The song was written in the mid-nineteenth century by Anton Gruber, a master composer from the Tyrol, whose work has since become a Christmas classic and translated into many languages.

During our stay at the Hotel Inglaterra, we became acquainted with a very pleasant Spaniard whose name I have unfortunately forgotten. This man had owned a wine cellar near Bilbao, only to lose it during the Spanish Civil War. He talked a lot to my husband and one day he invited us to visit all that was left of what had once been a wine-producing enterprise of some importance. I turned down the invitation because it was too cold to take Carlos out and I did not want to leave him in someone else's care at the hotel. But my husband decided that he would visit the cellar so as not to offend this man. When they got there, the Spaniard gave him a bottle of wine that had been aged for nearly 100 years, so that we might make a toast to our freedom and our future when we got to Argentina. That bottle of wine was very significant in our lives and later I will explain how we were often on the verge of uncorking it yet did not, postponing the moment as though with each postponement we could prolong our expectations of happiness. That was the second important bottle of alcohol in our lives. The first one – the bottle of cognac that got the SS official drunk on the train ride from Prague to Paris – had saved our lives. This second bottle was for celebrating the life that the first bottle had saved.

In Bilbao, I was able to send a telegram to my parents to tell them we were safe and sound in Spain, though penniless. They had very little money, but managed to wire us around 150-200 dollars. Part of that money enabled my husband to return to Irún and get back the watch he had pawned when we first arrived in Spain. I had worn that Omega watch when Carlos was born so I could keep track of my contractions before the delivery, and I still keep it with me. It had a special meaning for my husband as well, for the same reason.

ONE MORE STAGE IN SPAIN: BARCELONA

We were waiting for the day of departure, which was scheduled for early February, when a letter arrived out of the blue telling us to go to Barcelona, as we would be boarding a ship there on January 15. We, therefore, packed again, said goodbye to the people who were closest to us, and took a train to Barcelona. The trip lasted all night long and it was grueling because the train had wooden seats with no upholstery, which made us feel the cold all the more intensely. Carlos was beginning to catch a cold; he started coughing, and by the time we arrived in Barcelona, he had a raging fever. We had no money for a doctor or even for medicine.

The place where we were staying, which was run by HICEM, was not exactly a hotel but a squalid hostel for migrants in transit, located on the fourth floor of a building in the port area. There was no elevator and they gave us an attic room with a slanted wooden ceiling that was covered in a fine layer of yellowish plaster, worn and cracked by the ravages of time and dampness. The wind and the cold came in through the cracks, making it quite inhospitable. A skylight let in some daylight, but at night, a sad little light bulb made a weak attempt at lighting up the room – which was already sad and dreary enough – highlighting the water marks from the rain and snow that slid down the walls after seeping in from the outside. The only furniture in the room was a bed that could not even accommodate two people, a threadbare mattress, one pillow and a single blanket that managed to be heavy without providing any warmth. There was a bathroom out in the hallway, but it had no hot water.

This dispiriting environment is where we spent our last three days in Spain on our journey to freedom. We were very distressed over Carlos' health because his temperature did not drop below 39 degrees. My husband went to see the hostel manager, who had his office in the same building, and was furious when he found the man in a very compromising position with his secretary. After berating him for his behavior, he demanded that this man send for a doctor, saying: "I will not allow my son, who could have died in a gas chamber in Germany yet managed to survive, to die because of your negligence here in Spain, where we came under the protection of the organization you represent and must respect. I demand that you find a doctor for my son straight away."

Soon after, my husband and the HICEM representative came with a doctor who carefully examined Carlos and diagnosed pneumonia. He gave us sulphonamide, which was the most efficient medicine against infections at that time in Europe. Penicillin, discovered in 1928 by the Scottish scientist Alexander Fleming, began to be commercially produced in the United States in 1943, but it was still not available to us. Two years later, Fleming and his colleagues Sir Howard Walter Florey and Ernst Boris Chain were awarded the Nobel Prize in Physiology or Medicine for their work in this area. Carlos slowly got better, but the doctor warned us that it had been a serious case of pneumonia and that the child's health would be delicate for a while, so that we should be careful to protect him from the cold.

Friday, January 15, 1943 came around. That was the day we were to board the *Cabo de Buena Esperanza* (Cape of Good Hope), an ocean liner flying the Spanish flag and built by the shipyard Ybarra that was a twin of the *Cabo de Hornos* (Cape Horn) on which my parents had traveled to Argentina. This was to be our ship's last trip to the Americas. War had come to the Atlantic Ocean in the shape of submarines and torpedoes, which made sailing very dangerous. As a result, transoceanic travel became more intermittent until it was suspended altogether.

We still had not recovered from the weariness of so many thousands of kilometers of travel, from so much effort to overcome the obstacles that got mercilessly in our way, and most especially from the distress over Carlos' illness. Nevertheless, placing our faith in God and our eyes on a peaceful future in Argentina, we went to the port, I pushing the stroller where our child sat wrapped in blankets, and my husband carrying the two small but heavy suitcases that made up our hand baggage. In the meantime, our trunk was being placed in the ship's hold, courtesy of HICEM. We had to board at 8.30 in the morning, so it was barely daylight when we left for the port. It was dreadfully cold and it was raining – a light, languid kind of rain that made everything seem gray and shiny, as if lit up by the relentless drizzle that almost brought some beauty to the landscape. Just like the day when we left Prague, we looked beyond the overcast sky and saw, inside ourselves, the shining horizon of a happy destination.

There were hundreds of men, women and children on the pier, organized into long lines, almost all looking humble and patient. They carried their belongings in shabby suitcases or bags, or else in boxes and packages tied with string, and they all anxiously awaited the moment when they would start boarding the ship. They were Europeans fleeing Europe, escaping, like us, from war, hunger and death. Most of them were not Jewish and there were several groups of Gypsies.

We took our places in the line, but soon the drizzle turned into a steady rain and because it was so cold, we asked to be allowed on board because of the need to protect the child – without mentioning his illness, out of fear that international safety guidelines might prevent us from traveling. We were almost immediately allowed on board and walked up the gangway. There was paperwork to fill out as well as a medical check, and during the following weeks there would be much discomfort and a few surprises in store for us.

The first formality to get through was the medical checkup. I was afraid that Carlos would cough in front of the doctor, which would give away the fact that he had pneumonia and had not fully recovered yet. I explained to him that he must not cough or else he would not be able to go to Buenos Aires to meet his grandparents. Even though he was so small, Carlos closed his mouth with the tips of his fingers, pressed his lips tight and did not cough once, which not only eased my mind but also filled my heart with tender feelings for him. We were then told we had to go to the steerage area of the ship. We had no idea what that was, and to our surprise it turned out to be an enormous space right above the hold, in one of the lower levels of the ship. This space was full of single beds that looked shoddy, with thin, dirty mattresses and no bed sheets or blankets. All the people standing in line outside would eventually fill up this gigantic, common dormitory. That was where we would live for the entire duration of the voyage, with no creature comforts other than one flimsy bed; we would be sharing an insufficient number of toilets; and would be exposed to theft, offenses, assaults, filth and infection. The cold was paralyzing and the air was foul. I realized that my son's delicate respiratory tract would not be able to withstand such an atmosphere and that I had to take him out of there as soon as possible. My husband was not with me because men and women had separate dormitories, which meant that I, alone, had to find a solution and fast – but I had a lot of practice doing just that.

The *Cabo de Buena Esperanza*, the twin of the *Cabo de Hornos*, which were both owned by the Spanish company Ybarra. This is the ship on which Ilse, her husband and their son traveled to Buenos Aires on the vessel's last transoceanic journey due to the dangers of war.

The *Cabo de Hornos*, the ship on which Ilse's parents traveled to Argentina and which reached the port of Buenos Aires on October 3, 1941. This photograph was kindly provided by Captain Aldazábal, an instructor at the National Nautical School, and is part of his "Ship Images" collection.

I went up to the main deck where the ship had its medical facilities. During our checkup, I had noticed a small infirmary used to treat any illnesses that developed during the crossing. I asked to speak to the head nurse to whom I explained the situation and told her that if she agreed to keep Carlos there for the entire trip, I would give her a very long turquoise necklace that had belonged to my Grandmother Mathilde. I had managed to keep the necklace because on the couple of occasions when the Nazis had seen it, they thought it was just worthless costume jewelry. I did not have to insist — she accepted and said she would take the child immediately. I gave her the necklace as agreed and for the entire trip Carlos remained in the infirmary, where he was well fed, warm and clean.

There were wealthy people traveling in first class — aristocrats, politicians and intellectuals who were all in full and happy possession of their advantageous conditions, while the other sections of the ship carried war fugitives tormented by fear, spent by pain and destroyed by anxiety. When all the different passengers were finally on board, we heard the deep, imposing sound of the ship's horn and a slight feeling of nausea indicated that we had left port. Barcelona's skyline got blurry in the growing distance, as though it were vanishing in the misty drizzle, until it disappeared altogether. The small dot that the Catalonian capital had been reduced to finally vanished in a maritime landscape of leaden skies and choppy seas. It was a little after mid-afternoon.

SAILING TO LISBON

For an entire week we sailed to Lisbon. Due to bad weather and low temperatures, we spent the entire time in that large area they call steerage — or between-deck — in unhealthy and unbearably overcrowded conditions. We were surrounded by people who spoke different languages and had different customs, and for whom maintaining personal hygiene — if indeed they had such a habit — was an almost impossible task because of deficient sanitary facilities as well as the absence of any private space.

I have one clear, unpleasant memory of that leg of the journey: There was an ageing, overweight Roma woman who spent almost the entire time combing her long hair to rid it of the disgusting vermin that nested there. We complained and a ship's officer came down to tell her that she must wash and clean up, to which she replied with great haughtiness that she was 60 years old and had never taken a bath in her life and was certainly not going to do so now, "even less so," she said pointing to me, "to make that woman happy." I had just made an enemy with whom I would have to share the same traveling space for a long time. Another disagreeable memory concerns the meals that were served on tin plates that looked old, dented and poorly washed. The food consisted of a few bits of vegetables, some noodles and pieces of dark, rubbery meat that floated around listlessly in an oily broth. Fortunately, we still had our suitcase with some of the cured Serrano ham, cheese and olives that the generous Spaniards had given us as a present and which had been preserved by the harsh winter cold.

On Thursday, January 21, at 10.30 on a bright, mild morning, we arrived in Lisbon. The sky was clear and the transparent air refracted the sunlight with such intensity that we had to keep our eyes half shut to avoid being dazzled by it. After spending such a long time under gray skies with constant rain and the feeling of being hounded day and night by danger and fear, the warm breeze of that splendid morning against our faces and sensing the peace of our surroundings was like being in heaven. We were gradually overcome by a stimulating feeling of well-being that almost felt like being drunk, and a mantle of oblivion seemed to descend between the painful past and this moment of sudden plenitude. We were thirsty for peace, and we had just found it.

Once the vessel had docked, we attempted to disembark and take a walk on land, but we were informed that officials from the Embassies of Czechoslovakia and Palestine[19] — there was still no State of Israel — were coming on board to see a child who had been saved from a certain death, like Moses in the waters of the Nile. Following the introductions and customary greetings, the members of the Jewish delegation handed us a sum of money, aware that refugees from war-torn countries were always short of everything and could use help. Later, these same people invited us to get off the ship with them and visit the headquarters of the Embassy of Free Czechoslovakia in Portugal. They chatted with my husband for a long time, asking him to tell them everything he knew about what was going on in the war zone. They were

19 Editorial note: British Mandatory Palestine did not have an embassy in Lisbon. The visitors to the ship could have been members of the Jewish organization HIAS-HICEM, the Joint Distribution Committee or the Refugee Relief Department of the Lisbon Jewish Community.

very keen to hear news about their colleagues who had taken refuge in London, where a government-in-exile had been set up under Dr. Edvard Beneš, the successor of Tomáš Masaryk who resigned as president of Czechoslovakia for health reasons in 1935. Beneš, who had been a pupil and a great collaborator of Masaryk's, stepped down in 1938 and went to live in Paris until 1940, when he moved to London. My husband, who was up-to-date on all political and war-related events, told the embassy representatives everything he knew and they took good note. The Embassy of Free Czechoslovakia also gave us money enabling our financial situation to improve noticeably, so we decided to go to a pastry shop and have a coffee with cream, a real treat after so many privations. We also bought cigarettes because I really enjoyed smoking, and food for the journey, since we had ample evidence that the fare served on the ship was truly inedible and our provisions were running out.

ON OUR WAY TO THE AMERICAS

We spent one day in Lisbon and left early the next morning. Since we were heading south it started getting warmer and I spent most of each day on the deck with Carlos. I had set up a large washbowl there, which the nurse who cared for him had lent me. I filled the bowl with water and it became a pool for my son to play in. Towards sunset, I also used it to give him a bath before putting him to bed. During the night and at meal-times, he was still cared for at the infirmary. Since the weather was warm even at night, my husband and I normally slept out on the deck to avoid spending time in the dirty, overcrowded area down below. The closer we got to the Equator, the hotter it became and more people decided to follow suit and take their mattresses up on deck for the night. We began spending time with a group of mostly young married couples, and the camaraderie made the inevitable boredom of life on a ship somewhat more manageable.

One day, there was a singular celebration called the "Crossing of the Line." The ship's crew told us that we could participate in this traditional event of "baptizing" the people who were crossing the Equator for the first time – by which they meant pushing them into the swimming pool. It was customary to dress up for the occasion, but this was tricky for us because between-deck passengers had very few clothes with them. However, the desire to have a good time stimulated our imagination, and by lending each other things, we all managed to come up with amusing costumes. I wore a black skirt and white blouse and a maid from first class lent me an apron and a cap, so that I looked like a maid myself. When we crossed the Equator, I was thrown head first into the pool and several other christenings were thus performed amid much laughter and celebration.

On reaching Trinidad, British sailors came aboard and began a search for six spies who were reportedly on the *Cabo de Buena Esperanza*. They started with first class and worked their way down all the ship's levels until they reached ours. When they saw our documents – including the permission to leave German-occupied territories dated and signed in Berlin – they focused on us and interrogated us over and over again. Someone told us we would probably be arrested and kept in port until the end of the war. My husband suggested they cable their own embassy in Buenos Aires to inquire about us. The reply came two days later, confirming that we were trustworthy people and should under no circumstances be taken for spies. However, during the interrogations, the English realized that my husband was an intelligent man who possessed valuable knowledge and information. They asked him to collaborate and he agreed to tell them what he knew about war-related issues. Among other things, he knew the location in Czechoslovakia of the V1 and V2 bombs, which the German government was building in none other than the secret basement of the Sköda truck factory in Bohemia. Soon after, the Allies bombed that location. Finally, after a week, a waiter, a couple traveling in first class and three passengers from second class were arrested on spying charges. Subsequently, the vessel cast off for Dutch Guiana [now Suriname] with a stop in Santos (Brazil), where a large cargo of coffee was loaded into part of the between-deck, our traveling quarters, and transported to Argentina.

With each passing day of this last part of the crossing, we grew increasingly impatient to reach our destination and stand on solid ground. It was not just about walking on continental land, it was about finally getting to a place where we had been focusing all our hopes, all our desires, all our young dreams. We needed to build a life defined by stability, permanence, lack of danger or fear, serenity and the promise of well-being. In other words, we needed to live in peace. Although, even if we found all of that, we would still have to make great efforts to adapt to the customs of a country that was entirely unknown to us, even if we already loved it. As for me, I would also have to break the language barrier so I could teach my child Spanish. The first step when we left Prague had been to speak to him more in German and less in Czech, so that he might at least understand his grandparents when they spoke to him. Despite the effort this entailed for such a small child, my poor boy responded enthusiastically to the training and he soon understood everything my husband and I said to him, while he was able to babble back a few words in German.

Finally, the last day of the voyage arrived. We were up early to get ready for our arrival and the reunion with my parents. For me, seeing my father again was especially important and besides, I was bringing him a reason to go on living and the gift of continuity: a grandson. We tidied ourselves up as best we could, given the precarious conditions of our traveling quarters, but I kept wondering about the impression we would make on one another after such a long time — not so much the chronological time but rather time marked by life on the edge of danger, death and deprivation in our case, and for them, time defined by distance, solitude and the absence of loved ones in a faraway (though blessed) land.

PART TWO

SOUTH AMERICA

AT LONG LAST, BUENOS AIRES

At nine in the morning on Monday, March 1, 1943, the *Cabo de Buena Esperanza* docked at the port of Buenos Aires, its final destination. It had arrived around eight hours ahead of schedule, which is why there were few people waiting for the passengers at the pier. We had made out the city's skyline from a distance and as the sun drove away the last shadows of dawn, its profile became sharper against a broad, flat, luminous horizon that was bathed in subtle, iridescent reflections created by the humidity – the common, frequent humidity of Buenos Aires that we would come to accept as a genuine feature of the city's climate. Choked with emotion, it looked to us like a magical city that shone out rays of hope. How hopeful we were! What optimistic plans we had! We simply assumed that in Buenos Aires, we would find everything we desired.

My parents and I had spotted each other from a distance and we began waving our arms in greeting. We were acting out a scene replayed many times at every harbor in the world when a ship comes in. It was an ordinary kind of event that has been photographed, painted and filmed hundreds of times. But to us, that moment when we were all reunited felt so special, so exciting and so unique! What a miracle! We were all safe, while millions of other beings, whether Jewish or not, were perishing in Europe under gunfire, inside extermination ovens, or consumed by hunger, cold and suffering. And among these victims there were people of our own blood.

When the gangplank was lowered I raised my son in the air and as I was walking down I tripped and almost dropped the child, but he instinctively grabbed my clothes and saved himself. Once on land, we hugged and kissed my parents, overjoyed at being together again. My father picked up Carlos and the child wrapped his little arms around his grandfather's neck, placed his cheek against my father's young face — he was still barely 48 — and as though they had known each other forever, Carlos said: "O, papa!" yielding with complete trust to this being who showed so much affection for him. Ever since then and for the rest of their lives, my father and his grandson loved and respected each other dearly. No common language was necessary for them to understand each other during those first few moments. They were simply united by love.

One of the people waiting for the passengers of the *Cabo de Buena Esperanza* was the grandmother of that young woman whose last name was also Kaufmann and who had given birth to a baby boy at the same hospital where Carlos was born. She had come in hope of finding her granddaughter with her husband and child — her own great-grandson — because she had read in the *Argentinisches Tageblatt* that the list of passengers aboard the ship included the engineer A. Kaufmann with his wife and child. That was us, of course, but she had been hoping it would be her own loved ones. She walked up to us and when she realized her mistake, she asked if we had any news of her granddaughter. I told her that I had briefly known her because she had left the hospital on the day that I had given birth to Carlos, and I had been assigned her bed. But given the special circumstances we were both going through, we had exchanged little more than a greeting and a few good wishes. My husband and I looked at each other meaningfully, but we kept quiet. We should not be the ones to tell this sad, distressed woman that we knew both mother and child had been sent to Theresienstadt, because something of such importance should always be communicated in an official way by the authorities in charge of such matters. She said goodbye sorrowfully and walked away. I do not think she noticed our own distress, but I had a knot in my throat that prevented me from being nicer to her. What I really wanted to do was to hug her and tell her how beautiful her granddaughter had been — tall, slim and very refined — and how happy she had been with her baby.

When that upsetting moment had passed, we felt happy again at being together and left the port area to go to my parents' place, a modest apartment on the ninth floor of Lavalle 357, a building that still stands, which housed many immigrants back then. Two bedrooms, a small living room, a simple bathroom and a plain kitchen without an icebox were the only amenities to be found. It was sparsely furnished with simple, poor-quality furniture, but it was beautiful to me, because it symbolized freedom, peace and the beginning of a new life.

My husband, our son, his stroller, the trunk with our bedclothes and other belongings, our small suitcases and I all piled into my parents' small apartment as best we could. We looked like an invading army in the middle of such a small dwelling where each item had its assigned spot and everything was rudimentary, to say the least. We kept discussing everything that had happened during our period of separation. To celebrate our arrival, my parents had ordered a special meal with traditional Viennese dishes fixed by an Austrian woman who had been living in Argentina for a long time. Undoubtedly, this was a significant financial setback for them, since they were still not making enough to earn a living, but it was not just about celebrating our arrival. We were celebrating being together again, being free and having a future ahead of us that we knew might be difficult but also wonderful.

It was very hot and every night we would stay up late talking, thinking back, exploring the possibilities this country had to offer, making plans. We had to get organized quickly, start looking for ways to make money, and think of our next steps so as to create a normal daily routine, which was something we had not had for a long time. I began by getting to know the area and very soon I felt confident enough to cross Avenida Leandro N. Alem, pushing Carlos' stroller. Already back then, this avenue was a wide two-lane thoroughfare with heavy traffic and at each crossing there was a police officer who directed the flow of vehicles by blowing on his whistle and waving them through with his arms. Each traffic controller stood inside a covered circular booth placed on a raised metal stand about a meter-and-a-half from the ground, which he had to climb up to using a stepladder. From there, he had a good view of the area under his control and he, in turn, was very visible due to his raised position, the white gloves and the false sleeves worn over the jacket, which were also white and held in place with rubber bands. It soon became a regular occurrence for me to cross the avenue at the officer's indication and go to a street market that was set up twice a week on one side of Plaza Roma. At this market it was possible to buy all types of fruit, vegetables, meat, fish (fresh, so fresh!) and other good-quality household items at low prices. To me, it was a cornucopia – not of gold coins, but of all that wonderful food that we had lacked in Prague since the Nazi occupation. Yet, despite the low prices, we had to be very careful with our purchases.

In the afternoons, when the market stalls had been cleared away and everything was clean again, I took Carlos to that same square so he could practice taking his first steps. It was there that my son learned to walk and he found his balance by going up and down the slight slope on the edge of the flowerbeds, holding my hand and laughing merrily, as if surprised at his own feat. Often, while shopping in the morning at the market in Plaza Roma or enjoying my son's first steps on the warm afternoons of that golden fall season whose placid glow I found surprising, I would think back to the days when I used to go to the square in Olmütz to weave dreams of love and later buy food at the morning market.

Three days after our arrival, my husband found a job that paid 200 pesos. We needed 300 to survive, but he accepted the position anyway because his common sense told him that 200 pesos was better than nothing, and that it would be a good springboard to find a better job that paid what we really needed.

AN UNEXPECTED EVENT

Autumn was drawing to a close and it would not be long before winter set in – which in the southern hemisphere generally begins in June. I had trouble accepting such a radical change since in the northern hemisphere, where we came from, this month marks the beginning of summer. I realized that when *Rosh Hashanah* came round in September and the traditional end-of-the-year Christian holidays, instead of snow, we would have heat. But the hardest thing for me to bear was the humidity of Buenos Aires and its high temperatures. We were used to dry, intense cold and heavy snowfalls, and that autumn in Argentina was especially humid and stifling to me.

On Friday, June 4, I woke up early as usual. I had to go to the market at Plaza Roma, which opened on Tuesdays and Fridays. Since we did not have an icebox, we had to carefully plan the perishable food we would buy so as not to waste what was so hard to come by. The housekeeping lessons that Berta had taught me as a child in Vienna were still helping me here in Buenos Aires, and I always thought of her with love and gratitude. As usual, I walked down calle Lavalle until I reached Avenida Leandro N. Alem. However, when I got to the corner of both thoroughfares, no more than 150 meters from our front door and across from Plaza Roma, I noticed something strange and alarming. The food stands were only partially up – or maybe they had been partially dismantled. The stand owners seemed disconcerted and were grabbing the fruit crates that should have been neatly on display, putting away the precarious canvas tops that covered the stands and stowing everything away in their carts amid great confusion. The serene, colorful scene that I enjoyed on my daily walks and grocery shopping expeditions was quickly fading away, its appearance and rhythm altered. Soldiers! I was seeing soldiers in uniform, horses, military vehicles, weapons…I thought I must be having a nightmare. My God! Again? Here, too? What about peace? Where was peace?

I still did not speak Spanish, so I could not ask any passersby what this thing was that looked so much like war on a smaller scale. On the other hand, people walking by also showed surprise and alarm at the sight and the soldiers began hurrying us all along – including me – with screams and gestures. I remembered the day when I saw Nazi troops enter Prague and I had stood with my back pressed against the wall to avoid being seen and prayed that nobody would notice me. I figured that whatever was going on here, it was neither war nor combat. Military maneuvers? That's what I wanted to think. But I soon discarded that option, too. There was little doubt that something unusual was happening or was about to happen. I turned around and headed home. The doorman was closing the building doors earlier than usual and he told me something I did not understand. I went up to our apartment and my husband, who was the only one of us who understood Spanish, had just found out that the army, led by General Arturo Rawson, had overthrown the Argentine government of Ramón S. Castillo.

Three days later, there was another surprising event. Another general named Pedro Pablo Ramírez – who, we later learned, had been the director of the Escuela Superior de Guerra military college between 1939 and 1941, as well as war minister under the deposed President Castillo from 1941 to 1942 – forced Rawson out and declared himself the new president of the republic. His war minister was another general named Farrell, who, in October of that year, would be appointed vice-president. A new chapter was being written in the young history of Argentina. It was a chapter full of olive green uniforms, Führer-style jackboots, breeches patterned after Nazi uniforms, caps with vertical visors, helmets and Mauser rifles that were clearly German-inspired. It was a military setup with which we were not unfamiliar. From that moment on, there would be a cascade of surprises, removals and changes in power.

Meanwhile, in our closed little world made up of my parents, my husband, my son and myself – five Jews just arrived from war-torn Europe – we observed, compared, feared and hoped that what had happened to us there, what we had just escaped from, would not happen all over again here.

HEALTH AND MONEY PROBLEMS

It had been a month since Argentina's institutional order had been altered by the military coup, but our ignorance of local politics, the lack of communication due to the language barrier and the continuous discoveries and adaptation efforts we were making in this new world made us involuntarily indifferent to the political and military events that made headlines in the dailies that only my husband could read. But these events also made it into the *Argentinisches Tageblatt*, the Buenos Aires German-language newspaper, which my father read for the rest of his life, and to which I myself subscribed a long time ago.

Our efforts were aimed at procuring domestic order so we could enjoy peace, economic security and some degree of comfort. The wages my husband was making at a company that answered to Schroders Bank in London were not enough to make ends meet. It was imperative to solve our economic problems, thus my father and husband talked, planned and tried to get in touch with people who might open up productive channels for them. My husband thought a lot, used his imagination and made suggestions. My father analyzed things, discussed their options and went straight to the facts. But his world had to speak German, which was not such a common thing back then in Buenos Aires, while my husband, who spoke so many languages – eight in total, including Spanish – had a wider range of possibilities, even if his introverted nature slowed him down when the time came for action.

We were busy making plans when I decided to leave my son with my mother one afternoon to join my father at the Richmond Café, a traditional establishment that is still located on calle Florida, between calle Corrientes and calle Lavalle, just 300 meters from our home. This was where he used to meet people who put him in touch with the local business world. For me, it was a celebration and for both of us, it was a luxury at this time of economic hardship to have a coffee mid-afternoon and take a stroll together along a few blocks of the city's financial area, my father's almost natural habitat.

We returned home feeling content and refreshed after allowing ourselves a peek at the magnificent display windows of the elegant stores that filled calle Florida back in those days: James Smart, Harrods, Le Faune, Marilú – their displays were particularly splendid – and Sporting Steeper. But a major problem awaited us at home. My son Carlos was crying desperately and showing signs of being in great pain; he had lost his pink glow and his skin looked greenish. We managed to get a doctor to see him and he discovered a considerable lump in his belly: It was a hernia. Unfortunately, the diagnosis was that it was already strangulated and Carlos required immediate surgery. He was admitted to the Clínica Bazterrica with help from the doctor, who obtained very favorable conditions for us, even though these were still far from affordable.

The surgery lasted until two in the morning and was a success. Carlos had to remain in hospital for four or five days. I stayed with him and the medical bills kept piling up. We were now faced with yet another problem: How to pay for the hospital treatment. While I saw to Carlos, my father moved heaven and earth within the limited circle of acquaintances he had made and managed just in time to put together enough money to pay the doctor's fees, the surgery and all the other related medical expenses. He had been able to collect an advance on his share of the profits from a silk thread import business venture in which he was participating. Fortunately, Carlos celebrated his second birthday on September 10 fully recovered from the operation. It took the rest of us longer to get over it. It had been a big scare and a great effort.

OUR FIRST APARTMENT

Our financial limitations and those imposed by the space in which we were living, which afforded little comfort or intimacy, were making life difficult. Therefore, my husband and I decided to look for a new apartment for the three of us. We eventually found one on the second floor of a building that still stands at 2955 Salguero, next to an Esso gas station on the corner of calle Salguero and Avenida del Libertador. Visiting my parents meant walking from the corner of Salguero and Libertador to Lavalle and Reconquista and back again, approximately a seven-kilometer trip on foot pushing Carlos' stroller, since I did not want to pay the tramway fare, no matter how cheap.

Our new home was even smaller than the one where my parents lived and it had no view onto the street, but we moved there in September or October of 1943, taking with us a bed, a crib and a closet. We had neither a table nor chairs, but the apartment did have a central electric icebox and that was a good thing because the hot season was coming up and it allowed us to keep our food in a hygienic place. We made a makeshift table out of a board that we placed on top of our suitcases and ate our meals there. We were poor but free and we were happy. Youth makes problems go away like magic, as if they were just a game. And we were so young back then!

Since our apartment was on a low floor and its windows faced what they usually call "an air and light well" – which, in this case, provided neither one nor the other because it faced a tall, bare dividing wall – I began taking Carlos out to a nearby square – ironically called Plaza Alemania or Germany Square – so he could be out in the open and meet other children with whom he could play and learn Spanish. I started to get acquainted with other young women who also took their children to the square and who, fortunately, included one or two who had also fled the war in Europe. Although I made an effort to understand the women who only spoke Spanish and to make myself understood by them, I must confess that when I was with the German speakers I felt much more relaxed. Nevertheless, I was making daily progress with the language out of the need to buy groceries – always in small amounts and at moderate prices – and thanks to my fledgling social life at the square.

As time went by, we started longing for things that would probably not even have entered our minds or bothered us at times of war. But such is human nature. A growing sense of sadness overcame me when I saw other women wearing new, fashionable clothes while I could not even afford a simple dress. I started desiring some of those trivial, superficial little luxuries that every young woman longs for. However, just when this was really beginning to bother me, my son asked me for a bicycle because he could see other children racing each other and organizing games together. So, my own desires were relegated to the back burner, because Carlos was the absolute priority. I became obsessed with his constant plea: "Mommy, buy me a bicycle. Mommy, buy me a bicycle." I understood his childish desire. I, who had had everything as a child without even having to ask for it, suffered because I could not give my son something so simple, but our financial situation made a bicycle seem like a top-of-the-range Mercedes Benz.

I analyzed the prices of the daily items we needed and tried to imagine what would happen if I tried to save a little here and there, but it was pointless – our income was so low that we had only just enough to live on and there was no room for saving. All my calculations were in vain and Carlos' bicycle would continue to be a dream that kept him anxious and me downcast. But it is a known fact that when a mother wants something for her child, God helps her find it and this is how God helped us: I found out that the woman who worked at the store where I did my shopping – a poor, hard-working woman – was pregnant and needed a baby carriage. She also had a bicycle that her older daughter no longer used and I had the baby carriage that Carlos, who was nearly three, no longer used either. The solution came easily – we traded items. For several nights, while Carlos slept, I quietly cleaned, fixed and repainted the bicycle so he would not find out about it until it was ready. When it was completely repaired, I placed it in a visible spot and when he woke up in the morning, he had a wonderful surprise waiting for him. He laughed, jumped, got on and off his "brand-new" bike and ran in circles all around it.

For a long time after that, every time he was playing in the square, he stopped when he came near me, got off what he considered to be a truly fantastic vehicle and gave me a hug and a kiss. He was enjoying himself and I was happy. It was unforgettable!

THE SAN JUAN EARTHQUAKE

In the evening of Saturday, January 15, 1944, a tremor shook away the heavy drowsiness caused by the scorching heat and in many parts of Buenos Aires hanging lamps swung from their hooks, objects fell to the floor and doors and drawers opened and shut without human intervention. We soon heard on the radio that the province of San Juan, in the area of Cuyo at the foot of the Andes, had experienced an intense earthquake measuring 7.5 on the

Richter scale, with the epicenter in the provincial capital. The first reports talked about a large number of dead and wounded, buildings in ruins, deep cracks in the ground and various other horrors. It was easy to imagine the nightmarish scene, with hundreds of people trying to help the thousands of wounded victims in the middle of the madness that comes with such disasters, struggling against the darkness at night, fearing the possibility of replicas, stumbling over the rubble, the corpses and the bodies of agonizing people, laboring under the heat and threatened by fire, by the natural gases seeping up from the cracks in the ground and by the tremendous lack of water.

For the next few days, the country talked about nothing else and the government announced the official delivery of aid packages for the victims. As for the citizens' response, the Argentine sense of solidarity mobilized doctors, nurses and religious and civilian volunteers who all made their way to San Juan any way they could and did all that was humanly possible to soothe the victims' pain, despair and panic and to reduce the risk of epidemics, infections and looting. Collections were taken up on the streets, inside houses of worship, at government departments, everywhere. There was an intense desire to help but it was poorly organized and the entire country was in mourning.

Later, there was talk about murky maneuvering when the time came to hand over the aid money to the victims and about politicians using the tragedy for their own partisan purposes. A certain Colonel Perón and an actress and singer named Eva Duarte, who was known to be his intimate friend, traveled to San Juan to hand out medicines, blankets and food that had been donated by many people, and promised to provide assistance to the victims. The vast amount of reports coming out of the area got mixed in with a wave of rumors, and all of it made its way to the Argentine and foreign news agencies, which in turn relayed the information to the rest of the media.

Amid the flurry of news, little attention was paid to the fact that on January 26, [1944], Argentina had broken off relations with the Axis, the name given to the 1939 military alliance between Germany, Italy and Japan. At first, this alliance was called the Rome-Berlin Axis, but eventually it simply became the Axis. One of the radio stations kept playing a military march that sounded very familiar to us, because it was the same one used by the BBC during the war to introduce its news bulletins – the ones we listened to secretly at the Hotel Flora in Prague. After the tune came an unmistakable voice that communicated breaking news with a nasal sound and a sensationalist tone.

It was Ariel Delgado, the newscaster of Radio Colonia, which broadcast out of Uruguay's Banda Oriental or Eastern Strip, across from Río de la Plata. Delgado provided the latest news not just about the San Juan earthquake, but also about the equally fragmented and shaky political and military situation in Argentina – and particularly in Buenos Aires – and he did so in an interesting and more trustworthy way than the news coming out of the local stations. Indeed, the military structure had created a climate of restricted freedom here and press freedom was affected first of all.

We were interested in everything that was going on in this country that was so new and so dear to us, but the urgent need to resolve our daily problems deprived us of enough time to analyze things the way we would have liked to. We simply listened to the news without paying too much attention most of the time; we received subliminal information without stopping to think about what we were hearing. All that superficial information created a foundation of knowledge – not a very solid one, I admit – which, once we achieved some degree of economic stability, we began analyzing from the unique angle of foreigners who had fled a war.

A BREATH OF LIFE

The year 1944 began with the San Juan tragedy, but there is something magical about this country that seems to underscore the ups and downs of life, as though it were a land blessed by God. Therefore, the pain of so much death was soon mitigated by an event that was full of life: The media reported that an Italian couple living in Argentina, Ana María Aversano and Franco Diligenti, had had quintuplets and that all the children – three girls and two boys – were in good health. The multiple birth had taken place on July 15 of the previous year, but the couple had kept it a secret for eight months, until the children were strong, because they knew that such a rare event would capture the imagination of society and the international media, leading many curious people, as well as journalists, to their door. The Diligenti couple wanted their children to grow up in the warmth, privacy and serenity of their own home.

In order to dispel any doubts regarding the multiple birth – events of this nature are always questioned – in April 1945, a court ruled that the quintuple birth was without a doubt legitimate. When the children were born, the Diligentis, who already had three children, were living at 1700 calle Tronador, but the considerable growth of their family compelled them to move to a larger house surrounded by gardens at 3500 calle Pampa, where a Korean school now stands. These homes were not far from each other, in a traditional residential neighborhood of Belgrano R. This is where María Cristina, María Ester, María Fernanda, Franco and Carlos Alberto grew up peacefully. When they were old enough to go to school they were all sent to different private institutions to reinforce their individual personalities. Later, they all graduated from different foreign universities. Back then, it was not frequent to see multiple births, unlike now, when fertility treatments have made them more common. There had been another quintuple birth in the United States – the Dionne sisters – but the Argentine case, which was handled discreetly at all times, was like a breath of life at a time of national sadness.

MORE GOVERNMENT CHANGES

In March 1944, there was another change in government. When President Ramírez stepped down, Vice-President General Edelmiro Julián Farrell took his place while the war ministry – and soon after, on July 7, the vice-presidency – was placed in the hands of Colonel Perón, the same man who was in San Juan after the earthquake with the actress Eva Duarte. This event marked the beginning of the vertiginous rise to power of Juan Domingo Perón and Eva Duarte in Argentina. It was also the start of a long period of political, legal, social and economic upheaval – a progressive succession of fragmented changes of direction – that built a real revolution. Two years after arriving here in search of peace and security, we had not only jumped from one military coup to the next, but had also seen the country adopt a completely different appearance that would continue to change in the following years. Despite all this, we continued to try to build an economic foundation that would afford us some peace of mind and a chance for our family to get on in life.

We were witness to this entire period of change in Argentina without being substantially affected by any of it, yet we could not help but notice certain similarities with Germany's far-right prewar politics. During General Farrell's term in office there were measures aimed at accentuating the feeling of nationalism, and although nothing could really surprise us in this regard after experiencing its maximum and cruelest form under Nazism, we took note of certain laws that were rather on the dictatorial side: Radio stations could not air foreign music and all its programs had to feature folk and traditional Argentine tunes; news bulletins had to be preceded by the sound of martial strains; and a decree passed on December 31, 1944 made religious education mandatory. Folkloric dancing became part of physical education class, while the nation's symbols were visible everywhere and military marches were played left and right. This was just the beginning and we knew for a fact how things might continue and how far they could go.

1945, A YEAR TO REMEMBER

The year 1945 was underway and in Europe the Allies were defeating the Axis armies on all fronts. The end of the war was near. On April 12, US President Franklin Delano Roosevelt died of a cerebral hemorrhage; on April 28, Mussolini and his lover Clara Petacci were shot by Communist partisans near Lake Como, and their bodies were hung upside down in public. Towards the end of that same month, on April 30, the man who had sustained the greatest defeat of all, Adolf Hitler, committed suicide in Berlin with his mistress Eva Braun. On May 7, the German armies surrendered unconditionally at Reims, in northern France, while in the Far East the city of Hiroshima was destroyed on August 6 by an atomic bomb. On September 2, Japanese diplomats surrendered to General MacArthur aboard the USS Missouri. It was the end of a cruel war that had lasted five years, eight months and six days, and which had claimed the lives of 45 million people — sheer madness!

These events shook the entire world, but perhaps the event that had the biggest impact on us was the opening of the Nuremberg trials on November 20, and the criminal prosecution of Hitler's followers who had failed to flee or take their own lives following defeat. They were the murderers of my beloved Grandmother Mathilde, sweet Aunt Alicia, little Veruska and millions upon millions of human beings who will be no more. Besides Nuremberg, the killers would also have to face Divine Justice. Of our entire family back in Europe, there was only Clara Kaufmann left — my husband's sister — and my cousin

Robert Elias. My dear Berta was also alive, but it was a long time before we knew that any of them had survived the horrors of war.

In Argentina, 1945 was also an eventful year. On June 10, all Argentines had to change their driving habits when a law went into effect forcing vehicles to drive on the right side of the road rather than the left, as the British still do. Road signs reading "Stay on your left" were replaced with signs reading "Stay on your right," and the country began importing vehicles with the steering wheel on the opposite side. Was this change to the right a symbol or a paradox?

It was in the realm of politics that events reached historical proportions that year. Colonel Perón – who had already been vice-president since July 7 of the previous year – was growing noticeably more popular, and his own sheen was beginning to make President Farrell seem dull by comparison. On March 27, showing chameleonic skill after a period in which the country had veered to the far right, Perón declared war on the Axis powers, completing the severance of ties begun by then-President General Ramírez's formal declaration of January 26, 1944. Subsequently, Perón won the support of the working classes by enacting social laws of great political and social relevance – extended retirement plans, guarantees against layoffs, bargaining agreements and so on – making it easier to create the CGT, a powerful trade union federation. These measures and the resulting changes in the political and social fabric of this young country triggered a reaction by the middle and upper classes, and in October the government slipped into a crisis. Perón was removed from office, arrested and sent to Martín García Island, in the Río de la Plata.

But it was not long before the classes that had benefited from Perón's changes, under the guidance of Eva Perón, began demanding freedom for the man who was fast becoming their leader. On October 17, after coordinating state and military support for Perón, Eva Duarte harangued the people she referred to as "*descamisados*" ("shirtless ones"), mostly workers from the capital's blue-collar neighborhoods and areas near Buenos Aires. Some of these supporters marched to the military hospital where the colonel had been admitted as a patient, while the great majority made their way to Plaza de Mayo and began chanting for him. Finally, at around 11 at night, Perón appeared on the balcony of the Casa de Gobierno, the seat of government. The crowd went wild with enthusiasm and cheered him for over ten minutes. After that, Perón delivered a speech in which he announced that he was resigning from the military to become just another worker. This announcement was yet another one of the coups de théâtre that Perón was so good at, and which earned him another giant ovation and the passionate devotion of the working classes.

I saw from the terrace of our apartment building in Salguero the march of the *descamisados* go down calle Libertad, which back then was still called Avenida Alvear, and down Avenida Figueroa Alcorta (then Avenida Centenario), heading for the city center. Most of them were shirtless and they were all fired up, yelling Perón's name to the beat of drums. It brought to mind images of the French Revolution that I had read about so often in my school books; I thought of the *sans-culottes*, and heard the emblematic chords of *Allons enfants de la Patrie* inside my head. We later heard that these singing and chanting marchers had used the ornamental fountains in Plaza de Mayo to refresh their tired feet and rest from the weariness of the march – it was an especially hot day and the distances were long. All in all, it was quite an unusual scene.

There was one man who stood out among the demonstrators – a unionist from the Beriso meat-packing district whose name was Cipriano Reyes. This man, who took credit for being the architect and organizer of the October 17 march, was later persecuted and jailed by the Peronist regime for almost the entire duration of Perón's term in office. Reyes allegedly said in his own defense: "I only created October 17. Later, everyone jumped on the bandwagon of Perón's success." Eight months later, on June 4, 1946, on the third anniversary of the 1943 revolution – the starting point for his meteoric rise to power – Perón became president of Argentina after winning the February 24 elections. On October 3 of that same year, his government decreed that every October 17 from then on would be a public holiday called "*Día de la Lealtad*" or "Loyalty Day."

The following years were very politicized and numerous changes and battles on the ideological, political and social fronts took place. The CGT got stronger, unions made themselves heard, there was talk about a "cattle oligarchy," and the slogan "Yes to espadrilles, no to books" was circulated. People spoke about "four for one," which was not exactly a mathematical formula, and an unthinkable sanctification was suggested by the phrase "tomorrow is Saint Perón." Meanwhile, Eva Duarte became María Eva Duarte de Perón and later Eva Perón, although she would go down in history simply as Evita, a nickname coined by her "shirtless ones." Politically, she was a strong woman, but physically she was already showing the strain, especially during a trip to Europe in June 1947 when she visited Spain and was awarded the Order of Isabel la Católica by Franco himself. Years later, Colonel Perón, who had asked for permission to leave the army on October 17, 1945 to join the working classes, put his military uniform back on and was promoted through the ranks to general, later climbing the successive hierarchies of brigadier general, major general and army general.

My husband, who was by nature a keen observer of world politics and social change, showed great interest in all this upheaval that had come as a surprise to us so early in our new Argentine life. Over the years, he continued to analyze Argentina's politics in his cold, objective way without ever renouncing his passion for the piano, which was his way of taking a break from the outside world. And, while these and other things were going on, we kept an eye on our expenses and tried to make progress through tenacity, thrift and daily effort. Meanwhile, my father was already on his way to recovering his former financial position. Everyone's major concern at that point was the education of my son, who symbolized the future and family continuity.

LIZY, A BUNDLE OF JOY

As Carlos got older, I felt an increasing desire to have a second child. I did not want my boy to be an only child like me, and besides, I really wanted a little girl. I had heard that the birth of a little woman always brings joy to any home, and I was sure that God would grant me such happiness. But time went by and I did not fall pregnant. We decided to see Dr. Otto Jürgens, a real authority in his field, who was then working as General Director of Hospital Alemán. Dr. Jürgens ran some tests and decided I needed to take medicine to regulate my hormonal balance, which was out of kilter after years of poor nutrition and great stress.

Not long after, we had our first victory: I was pregnant. The second victory came on January 16, 1948, in the shape of a pink, blonde, soft and serene little girl whom we named Alicia in memory of my dear aunt. Just like Carlos, Alicia – Lizy – weighed two kilos and 750 grams at birth. Everything about her birth was good and sweet and happy. Everything that came later was, and continues to be, a source of joy and pride for me because of her kindness, her bright intelligence, her love for me and her sense of responsibility. Lizy – the wanted child and the desired daughter. Lizy – my great friend. The distance between Madrid and Buenos Aires has not been able to defeat us: The telephone and lately, the fax machine, keep us together nearly every day, even if month after month we are shocked at the hefty telephone bills that bear witness to our long conversations and our desire to remain united.

As soon as Lizy was born and even before she had been completely cleaned and dressed, a nurse took Carlos to a room next to the delivery room so he could look at his sister. When he saw her, Carlos asked what "that" was. When he was told that "that" was his sister, he replied that he wanted a brother so they could play together. However, when Lizy and I were settled in a hospital room, Carlos began caressing her and saying that he loved her and would always take care of her. He was never again jealous and they were always very close and loved each other deeply. Carlos was barely six-and-a-half when Lizy was born.

Carlos and Lizy were born at completely different times. Carlos came into the world during the Nazi occupation, in a hospital where Jews were discriminated against, at a time of shortage and danger and with the extermination camp as our nearest destination. Lizy was born in a peaceful Argentina, at the excellent Agote clinic, surrounded by comfort, amenities and gifts. Our economic situation was stable and it was an especially significant time for us Jews, because on May 14, 1948, the world witnessed the creation of the State of Israel. Then, in 1949, Ben-Gurion, who had fought so hard for this dream, would obtain a new triumph before the eyes of the world: forming a government in Israel.

By then, my father had been able to build himself a house in San Isidro that was surrounded by a beautiful park. Lizy spent long hours in her carriage under the shade of its trees and Carlos liked to swim and play in the pool. For many years after Lizy was born, we spent the summer months and various other weekends there with friends and family. It was our new Veilchen Villa.

The constant effort my husband and I made to improve our situation started to pay off. We were able to move to a better location and rented a seventh-floor apartment that was more comfortable, better ventilated and had more natural light. This building still exists on calle Salguero, between Castex and Gelly, around 70 meters away from our first apartment. That was where Lizy had her own room fitted with the kind of colorful children's furniture that was available in Buenos Aires but which Carlos had not been able to enjoy. I

Winter and summer at the San Isidro country house.

was buying myself fashionable dresses, good clothes and shoes for the children, and giving them toys that made them happy. Carlos, and years later Lizy too, went to a good elementary school. They had friends, went to parties and had happy childhoods. We were beginning to be ourselves again.

THE YEAR OF THE LIBERATOR GENERAL SAN MARTÍN

The year 1950 came round and we discovered that it marked the hundredth anniversary of the death of General San Martín, the nation's greatest hero and its liberator during the years when Latin American countries were struggling for independence from Spain. Although we knew that General José de San Martín was dear to Argentina, Chile and Peru — the three countries that owe their independence to his brilliance and heroism – we could not help but notice how much attention the government lavished on every last detail of the program in honor of the "Libertador." Possibly the one detail that struck me the most was the obligation to begin every single official notice, news publication or school report with the phrase "Year of the Liberator General José de San Martín" right after the date. Carlos, who was then nine years old, had to follow this rule when he did his homework. Over the course of that year many tributes were held, monuments inaugurated and street and place names changed. This was the year when Avenida Alvear became Avenida del Libertador José de San Martín, which was later shortened to the more practical name Avenida del Libertador.

The main tribute was held on August 17, exactly 100 years after the death of San Martín in voluntary exile at Boulogne-sur-Mer in northern France. I remember there was a spectacular military parade down the avenue that was to take his name. Perón was part of the parade, riding his famous pinto horse that he called "El Mancha" (The Stain). He arrived at the presidential box in this fashion and at three o'clock – the time when San Martín had died 100 years earlier – he gave the order for the Caura bell to toll – a bronze bell that had been shipped in from Peru because it was the same one that had announced the death of the Liberator in 1850.

We watched the parade from our apartment on Salguero and Castex with some friends who came over for the day. All the buildings back then were low and from our seventh-floor balcony we could see Plaza Alemania, where I took my children to play, the entire Avenida Alvear, Avenida Figueroa Alcorta, the Monument to the Spaniards, the trees of Tres de febrero Park, and Río de la Plata to the east. Everything between the river and ourselves was built low and we could also make out the railroad tracks of Ferrocarril Mitre, Central Argentino and the Buenos Aires Al Pacífico.

POLITICAL CHANGE WAS IN THE AIR

The year 1951 was barely underway when my husband, who was a sharp observer and possessed an uncanny knack for detecting political or social change, began to notice a certain decline in power. Several strikes were held that ended in violence, leading to the application of martial law. At the same time, there was an attitude of obsequiousness towards Perón and Eva that became more apparent with each passing day and could mean nothing good. Everything that was inaugurated, whether it was a street, a building, a square or a bridge, was dedicated to the couple and bore their names. Growing inflation was destabilizing the national economy and eroding private savings, putting Argentines in a position they had never before had had to face. Most did not know how to defend themselves from the sudden and growing devaluation of their currency and their assets. Luckily, this problem did not affect us greatly for two reasons: First, we already had experience when it came to uncontrolled inflation and what it meant, since we had lived in pre-war Europe; and second, we had neither assets nor savings that could lose their value. That is, even though we had made some progress, my husband and I were still poor.

Perhaps the most significant sign of destabilization was the closing down of the newspaper *La Prensa* on January 26. Later, the assault on *La Nación* would come as well as the closing down of *La Vanguardia*, Argentina's traditional Socialist daily. Several regional magazines and daily and evening newspapers from Buenos Aires were suspended and restrictions on press freedom also reached radio stations and film newsreels such as the weekly *Sucesos Argentinos* and the film industry. To top it all, newsprint was rationed.

On August 22, 1951, with elections coming up, the CGT — the powerful union that Perón set up and whose support he could always count on — proclaimed the presidential formula "Perón-Eva Perón." But on August 31, Eva declined to be part of the tandem and everyone could see that she was extremely pale, weak and spiritually broken. The rumors about her illness were thus confirmed: She had cervical cancer. The kind of therapy and preventive checkups that save so many lives these days did not exist back then. The exhaustion she had felt on her trip to Europe was the first symptom of the danger lurking beneath the surface, but caught up in the frenzy of work, she ignored the signs. She had less than a year left to live. In October, Eva Perón's book *La razón de mi vida* (The Reason for My Life) was published and became a mandatory textbook in schools during Peronism. My own children had to use it in class.

In 1951, a truly important event for the country and for the media took place: the first television broadcast. Even if it was just a privileged few who were able to enjoy such a momentous event, it was the first step towards Argentina's current television network. The first images that were seen on Buenos Aires television sets were shots of the celebration of Loyalty Day in Plaza de Mayo, on the sixth anniversary of October 17, 1945. Peronism was undoubtedly in full swing in Argentina. There were just over 300 television sets in Buenos Aires at the time, all of them imported, and the broadcast emission barely reached beyond the Federal Capital. Naturally, there were still no such things as relay antennas.

FAMILY LIFE

We led a family life. My father's financial situation had greatly improved and he proved it with gifts for the children and also for me. My husband was working at Casa Iturrat and earning enough to put our minds at ease with regard to money matters. This allowed me to buy Carlos a television set that ended up providing entertainment for the entire family, especially when bad weather forced us to cancel our plans for outdoor walks. I was able to buy that television set, which I paid for in several installments, not only thanks to our improved financial position, but also to the sale of a wristwatch.

Our family always enjoyed the classic "five o'clock tea" at the San Isidro country house. **From left:** Adalbert Kaufmann, Carlos (aged eight), Ilse, Karoline Hahn, Paul Hahn and little Lizy.

I was still entirely devoted to caring for my family and keeping house. Carlos was going to school, Lizy was growing up happy and we were permanently in touch with my parents. We always spoke German as a family, but the kids also spoke Spanish. Carlos was learning it at school and Lizy at the square, and both of them practiced it with their father. I learned it partly from them and partly out of the need to communicate with the people in my immediate surroundings.

My father began having social commitments as a result of his business dealings, generally with foreigners passing through Argentina on commercial or diplomatic missions, or else with people who were settling there. At such times, I went over to my parents' house – they had moved to a building on 2737 Malabia, where they rented the third floor – and I prepared a proper reception for the guests with hors d'oeuvres and cocktails, a full meal including fine desserts, plus coffee and sweets. I did all this work out of love for my father, so he would feel my presence and support. Again, I applied the lessons and skills taught to me by Berta regarding optimal organization of time and proper food selection.

My parents had rented the apartment on calle Malabia – now called calle República Árabe Siria – from Doctor Ernesto Pittaluga, a man with a wonderful family. The Pittaluga children and my own kids became friends from a very young age. They and Carlos remained friends until his death, and their friendship with Lizy has endured over the years. They also continue to visit and spend time with me. We all feel a sincere affection for each other, and I consider them part of the family. I still keep the lease my parents signed on that apartment and which was renewed every two to three years until my father's death. My widowed mother then expressed her desire to live alone in the apartment, which she did until she was too old to fend for herself. After which, she came to live with us until her own death.

MOURNING AND MYTH

July 1952 came round. Since late September 1951, Eva Duarte had remained in bed, cut off from all her activities and rapidly getting weaker. She fought against death for ten months while the CGT and other sympathetic groups led renewed efforts to show their support through all sorts of tributes despite the lugubrious climate. She only left her sickbed to stand next to Perón when he took office as president for his second mandate on June 4, 1952. When she stepped onto the balcony of the Casa de Gobierno her body, consumed by the awful illness, seemed lost among the folds of an enormous fur coat and her face was pale and gaunt. She was leaning against her husband for support, and it was there that she received the last tribute of her life. It was for her, more than for him, that the people – her people, as she called them – were cheering. She turned towards Perón looking for support, even as she tried to conceal her tears, but the ever-alert photojournalists captured the moment in an explosion of camera flashes and turned it into one of the historic photographs of the era – one that marked the end of her reign, which continues to be controversial to this day. Watching her on television, even her adversaries grieved for her.

Eva Perón died at 8.25 on the evening of July 26, 1952. She was 33 years old. The announcement was made on the radio stations of Radio del Estado and Cadena Nacional de Radiodifusión. The wake was held at the Labor Ministry, in the building currently occupied by the Legislature Palace of the Government of the City of Buenos Aires, on Diagonal Sur. For several days, the roads and sidewalks around the building were covered with hundreds of floral tributes piled on top of each other, with no distinction as to the name or hierarchy of the person who had sent each one. The tributes to Eva Perón continued later in Congress. I do not recall exactly how long all these ceremonial activities lasted, but I would say close to 15 days.

During all this time, regardless of the cold and the rain, there were long lines of people – sometimes stretching as far as ten blocks – who wanted to pay their final respects and also those who simply wanted to see her body, which had been prepared for public display. Finally, her body was taken for embalming by Dr. Ara, a Spaniard hired by the Peronist government. Eva Perón's remains were transported with top honors inside a coffin resting on a cannon gun carriage and covered with an Argentine flag. We all watched it on television. I had never seen anything like it, and I doubt anyone else had, either. But her mortal remains did not have an easy trip to their final resting ground. After several politically motivated moves that were carried out with the utmost secrecy, Eva Perón's body undertook a long journey and finally wound up in a Milan cemetery, buried under a false name. The exact location was a mystery to most and a well-kept secret by the few people in the know.

It was not until 1971 that the traveling corpse was returned to Perón on orders of the government of General Lanusse. By then, Perón was living in Spain, in an elegant residential area outside Madrid known as Puerta de Hierro, in a mansion that he named "Quinta 17 de Octubre." His wife's body remained there for a long time until it was finally brought back to Buenos Aires and buried at La Recoleta, the most aristocratic cemetery in all of Argentina.

Adored and despised like few other people, Eva Perón was a self-proclaimed "champion of the working classes" who commissioned tailor-made outfits from Europe's most expensive designers and had them flown over to Argentina. She was born poor and died powerful, and her body, which received all kinds of state honors, was finally buried next to those of her fiercest opponents — the richest and most aristocratic members of Argentine society. Today, Eva Perón is a legend whose life is depicted in an opera, several films and a myth that survives somewhere between love and hate, between memory and oblivion.

THE VIOLENT YEARS

We thought that things would calm down after the mourning was over. We were not really afraid of this succession of political and revolutionary events that we had been observing since June 4, 1943, but certain similarities with our own experiences in Europe before and during the war made us feel that we should keep a close eye on the political situation. We had observed on several occasions how the right made apparent turns to the left in order to gain popular support; there was a lack of freedom — we were especially alarmed by the lack of press freedom — and a clear favoritism towards followers of the regime, while opponents were persecuted. All that, set against a backdrop of clear antisemitism, created a situation that made us watchful, if not fearful.

We remembered the encounter aboard the train from Dresden to Paris with the Nazi official and his wife who were going to France on their honeymoon — the same official who drank the bottle of cognac to alleviate his toothache; the same one who confidently stated that Germany would win the war and then take over Argentina. We put two and two together and began feeling concerned. Carlos was starting to prepare for his *Bar Mitzvah* and needed to begin his religion studies. To avoid his having to go to the synagogue on calle

Libertad, in the city center, we decided to hire a private tutor who came to our house twice a week and tried to ensure that Carlos would never feel unsafe or persecuted. Lizy was still too young to notice.

In April 1953, a terrorist group detonated two bombs in a public rally at Plaza de Mayo. The protesters cried "*leña, leña*" ("let's give them some stick"), while Perón himself egged them on, and soon after they torched the headquarters of several political groups, including the Socialist Casa del Pueblo, the Casa Radical and the magnificent Jockey Club building, which housed a very valuable library. This episode was followed by more violent acts of varying intensity, which in 1954 finally crystallized into a systematic campaign of violence against the Catholic Church, followed by more protests and public disturbances. Due to our concern I tried not to go to the city center because it did not feel safe there anymore. Meanwhile, I worked on Carlos' *Bar Mitzvah* ceremony, which made me happy, although I never stopped worrying about what was going on all around us.

CARLOS' BAR MITZVAH

When he turned 13 in 1954, and after studying religion for two years, Carlos was ready for his *Bar Mitzvah*, the ceremony in which a Jewish male formally accepts his responsibilities towards God, religion and life, and which confirms the Hebrew name he received after his circumcision, a week after birth. But it so happened that we had been unable to have Carlos circumcised eight days after his birth, because the Reich had not only made it mandatory for Jews to wear a yellow badge with the Star of David, as I explained earlier, but had also prohibited circumcision in all occupied territories.[20] In Prague, the only rabbi who was authorized by religious leaders to perform this rite had been sent to a concentration camp and never returned.

Eight days before the *Bar Mitzvah* ceremony, which was set for Saturday, September 18, 1954, an employee from the temple on calle Libertad went to my husband's office to ask about Carlos' Hebrew name. My husband explained

20 Editorial note: Circumcision was not prohibited; however, in some parts of Eastern Europe Jews were prohibited from giving birth, as in the Shavli Ghetto.

that we had been unable to perform the circumcision rite and that, as a result, Carlos did not have a Hebrew name. This created a huge problem. I received a telephone call from the rabbi and soon thereafter another one from Carlos' private tutor. They were both furious and told me in no uncertain terms that if the child was not circumcised he could not have his *Bar Mitzvah*, because religion did not permit a Jewish male to be presented in such conditions before the Torah.

In desperation, I went to the temple on calle Libertad, where the ceremony was supposed to be held. I asked to speak with the top rabbi and I explained to him that Carlos was born in Prague during the Nazi occupation and in adverse circumstances that made circumcision impossible, and that his life had been in danger several times, but that he had been miraculously saved. But the rabbi dryly told me: "Impossible. Get that idea out of your head." To which I firmly replied: "Now you listen to me, Rabbi. Nobody in my family ever changed his religion. We were born Jewish and we will die Jewish. In our generation, almost all our relatives were cremated in extermination camps for being Jewish. My son was miraculously saved from being taken to the gas chamber because God willed it so. Now he is happily awaiting his *Bar Mitzvah*, but you won't allow it! You don't want to understand the reasons why he could not be circumcised, so to me you are worse than the Gestapo! If my son cannot have his *Bar Mitzvah* as he wishes, I will go to the nearest church and have him and myself baptized." The rabbi was impressed by my speech and promised to call a meeting of the Temple Council to analyze the case. At 11 o'clock that same night, he phoned and said: "Madam, your motherly love has won out. I congratulate you. For the first time ever, we are going to allow a child in front of the Torah under these conditions." There was an explosion of joy at home when I told Carlos about the council's decision.

On the day of the ceremony, all our friends were at the synagogue. Sitting in the front row was Ambassador Brunel, Carlos' godfather. It was very moving to have him with us on such an important occasion, because he had always represented aid, salvation and support – he was a true friend who had never hesitated to protect us every time we had been in danger and every time we had had to act to save our own lives. Once the ceremony was over, and before being congratulated by the guests, Carlos came up to the section of the temple reserved for women and gave me an excited hug, saying: "Mommy, thank you so much for everything you've always done for me. Thanks to you I've had my

Bar Mitzvah and thanks to you I will now have my party!" Carlos was later congratulated by everyone at the temple and had a beautiful party at the Alvear Palace, the nicest and most luxurious hotel in Buenos Aires. We were thrilled and satisfied at all this happiness that God was bestowing on us as compensation for all the suffering and hardship of the past. We thought of uncorking that bottle of wine that had been a gift from the cellar owner in Bilbao, but we decided to wait for another occasion that was not linked to religion.

Life went on. Our children grew up, studied and became better people through personal effort and dedication. Lizy, who at first was not a good student, one day told me: "I am a bad student now, but in six months I will be at the top of my class, because you are making the effort to send us to a good school that is very expensive, and I must return the love you are showing us." And she was as good as her word. She was not only the best student in elementary school, but also in high school and college. We were content. Our children were growing up happy and healthy. They were proving to be responsible kids who understood the efforts their parents were making to give them a life full of love and hope for the future. And for us it was a relief that this was so.

ANOTHER YEAR OF UNCERTAINTY

On the political front, 1955 was a violent year. The Perón government took several aggressive measures against the Catholic Church and the political climate became very tense. Among other things, Perón eliminated the religion classes that he had once made mandatory, and he began persecuting certain priests. On June 11, the day of Corpus Christi – a very important celebration in the Christian calendar – Mass was held at the Metropolitan Cathedral and was attended by so many faithful that people had to stand outside the temple, braving the cold and filling up most of Plaza de Mayo. Suddenly, there was an outbreak of rioting by a group of activists who ransacked businesses, attacked embassy buildings and burned an Argentine flag. On the afternoon of the following day, after Sunday Mass was over, a group of government supporters launched an assault against the cathedral and a pitched battle ensued when the congregation attempted to defend their church.

Four days later, on Thursday, June 16, the Argentine Navy and Air Force bombed Plaza de Mayo in an operation that was generally deemed thoughtless, unexpected and unwonted in this city and country that were so peaceful. The passersby who happened to be there, mostly local workers having lunch or people on errands at the nearby banks, were the innocent victims of this failed air strike that did not yield the desired result: to eliminate Perón. The damage to the buildings around the square is still visible and bears witness to a revolutionary attempt that went down as sheer madness after causing death and destruction, yet failing to achieve its goal.

That night, the same groups that had attacked the cathedral now launched what they called "Operación Hoguera" (Operation Bonfire), setting fire to around ten churches, including some that contained valuable relics and which were housed in beautiful, historical buildings such as Santo Domingo, San Francisco, San Ignacio and San Miguel. The bishop of this latter church, Monsignor Miguel de Andrea – a known regime opponent – was arrested before the fire broke out by the area's police commissioner and taken to police headquarters for protection, since the police knew ahead of time what was going to happen and that the firefighters would not arrive in time to put out the fire. The damage was extensive and so was society's dismay, regardless of individual religious beliefs. The Vatican excommunicated the perpetrators, and Perón was one of them.

LIZY AND HER DOLLS

On Thursday, June 16, 1955, I was downtown with Lizy picking up a couple of dolls that we had left at two stores that specialized in fixing broken toys. First, we went to calle Florida to retrieve her Marilú – a classic Argentine doll that brought happiness and entertainment to generations of girls. Then we went to San Martín and Viamonte, where we picked up her Mariquita Pérez, a Spanish doll that made its appearance on the market much later than Marilú and was trying to compete with it. Suddenly, we heard the roar of engines in the sky and everyone on the street looked up in confusion. There were naval planes and they were flying low. Alarm spread like wildfire and desperately people began running for cover as businesses shut their doors and pulled down their blinds to prevent looting, which was not an uncommon occurrence at the time.

I remember picking up Lizy, who was holding both her dolls. I started running, but she was already seven years old and even though she was small, after a few meters I realized I was not as strong as I thought I was. I put her down and told her that we had to run together. I took one of her dolls to make her carry less weight, pulled her Tyrolese hat down tight, did the same to myself, and we made our panicked way to Avenida Córdoba, where vehicles were going by full of people fleeing the city center. We had just run across calle Suipacha when a car stopped – no doubt because of the Loden jackets and Tyrolese hats we were wearing – and its driver asked us in German where we were going. "Towards Palermo," I said in a scared voice. "Get in, I'll take you there, I'm going to Belgrano," replied the driver. Showing a great sense of solidarity, this kind man took us all the way home, which was a huge relief to me physically and emotionally because I must confess that on that day I relived the fear that the war had burned into me.

Three months later, on Friday, September 16, the Revolución Libertadora (Liberating Revolution) broke out in three places. Perón's government declared a state of siege and imposed a curfew. Everything became very confusing and Radio Colonia kept broadcasting news from Uruguay that contradicted the information aired by local stations. On Sunday, June 18, the navy positioned its ships on Río de la Plata with the aim of bombing the oil refineries on its shores. We were very afraid that night, because back then there was nothing standing between our building and the river that might protect us in the event of an explosion. Sitting on the seventh floor of Salguero and Castex, we felt like an easy target.

At two in the morning on June 19, Dr. Pittaluga phoned to say that he was coming to pick us up and taking us to my parents' place, where we would be safe. We organized the move quickly and went there with the kids, a few necessary clothes and very shaky nerves. The situation eventually calmed down, but it was a few days before we returned home because these events coincided with *Rosh Hashanah*, and my parents asked us to stay long enough to share the main ceremonies.

The revolutionary forces finally won and on Friday, September 23, General Eduardo Lonardi, who had led the uprising since its beginnings in Córdoba, arrived at Buenos Aires' small airport to take over the government. A rejoicing crowd followed him to the Casa de Gobierno and cheered him from Plaza de Mayo. We saw the throngs of people celebrating his victory from our seventh-floor apartment.

Perón, defeated and deposed, negotiated his departure and fled to Paraguay on a gunboat. It had been 12 long years since June 4, 1943. We all yearned for some peace and quiet and political stability — an elusive wish for Jews and also for Argentines. We trusted it would come, we willed it to do so, but the times ahead were not to be as quiet as we would have liked. The displaced Peronists did not yield their power and prerogatives easily and a weakened, hurt and disorganized nation stumbled forward, dodging obstacles on its search for that "destiny of greatness" that had been so often promised and so often postponed, so frequently sought after but so hard to find. Just as with people, countries need a period of convalescence after a bout of sickness; they need to mourn their dead and they need some sanity after so much madness. We were on our guard, and because we had learned our lesson early on, like the prophet Daniel, we kept working, watching our few belongings and being careful with our money.

THE SCOURGE OF POLIOMYELITIS

The year 1956 had barely begun when there were several recorded cases of poliomyelitis in the area of San Martín, very near Buenos Aires. In just a few weeks the disease had spread to the rest of the province and then all of a sudden there were cases throughout the country. The outbreak had all the signs of an epidemic. School classes were suspended and we women looked insane as we cleaned our houses like mad with the few disinfectants that were available on the market. Homes smelled like carbolic acid and children smelled like camphor because of the little bags containing this product that hung from their necks. Apartments were scoured with bleach, and all fruits and vegetables were boiled, without exception. Hands were not just washed but scrubbed with soap, shoes were left outside and bed sheets and towels were washed with bleach and ironed at top temperature, to the point that they nearly burned. These were all commendable measures, but today we know that they were not a truly effective way of preventing contagion.

Faced with these perils, we decided to isolate the kids from the outside world. We moved to the weekend house in San Isidro and stayed there with my parents until the danger was over. It was not easy spending several months in this self-imposed confinement during which nobody came in or out of the house except my husband, who continued to go to work, stopped by my father's office in Buenos Aires, and came to be with us on weekends. Without help from any maid, I cooked, cleaned, ironed and kept the children entertained when they got sad or bored because they could not see their friends. My parents, particularly my father, helped with this task by playing chess, Ludo and Monopoly with them and telling them stories. Our only connection with the outside world was the telephone.

Everybody still had fresh memories of the 1953 polio epidemic, which had mostly affected children under four years of age. Many of them had died and others had suffered the consequences for the rest of their lives, becoming invalids without any hope of recovery. In mid-September, for the first time, schools and health centers began administering a polio vaccine developed by a US bacteriologist named Jonas Edward Salk. His research into the prophylaxis of polio yielded the Salk vaccine, thus named in his honor, and the effectiveness of which had been announced in the United States in April 1955. When the epidemic subsided in May, we returned to Buenos Aires and started reorganizing our lives. I already had a lot of practice with that.

MY FATHER'S BUSINESS

Five years after the war in Europe ended, through his commercial relations with a firm called Stines, my father got in touch with the German company Thyssen. Times had changed and so had the people who ran Thyssen, who had once been Nazi sympathizers. With the war over, Germany was reorganizing itself and what businesses really cared about was effectiveness, honesty and personal ability, not race or the beliefs of the people working for them. Under these circumstances, my father, Paul Hahn, was offered the chance to be Thyssen's representative in Argentina. This was not just a great opportunity for him because of the advantageous working conditions, but also as a Jew he felt proud of the fact that he was selected for the job, which he carried out until his death.

Some time earlier, my father and my husband had imported a road-making machine – an investment that had used up almost all of their savings. As time went by they found themselves unable to sell the machine, which caused them great distress as they needed to recover their investment in order to honor certain financial obligations. In what turned out to be a stroke of good luck, they finally agreed to rent it to provincial authorities that showed an interest in the machine and eventually purchased it after seeing how well it worked. From that moment on, my father and husband continued to import road machinery. Not only was this enterprise very successful, they also had the satisfaction of seeing it lay down the kilometers of asphalt that brought the provinces and ports closer to the capital. These were the development years under President Arturo Frondizi.

In 1960, Carlos, who was already 19 years old and had begun his engineering studies, learned how to operate and maintain the machinery from a technician that my father's company had flown over from Germany. Carlos learned how to operate a fire extinguishing system called Unimoc, which was also imported by my father and husband. The main element in this system, which was then being used at airports around the world, was a chemical foam that expanded quickly on contact with air and immediately put out the fire. Perhaps the systems currently used at airports are derived from that original Unimoc.

When these devices were introduced in Buenos Aires and presented on the premises now occupied by the Sheraton Hotel – but which then housed the Parque Japonés, a famous amusement park – Carlos was put in charge of demonstrating how they worked, and he undertook this task earnestly and with a great sense of responsibility. At one point during the demonstration, Lizy, who was very short in stature and also very short-tempered, ran towards her brother as he was explaining how the fire extinguisher worked, grabbed one of the hoses and began taking part in the demonstration without anybody's permission, drawing smiles from the audience. The demonstration was broadcast on television because it was such a novelty, but despite that, only one unit was sold. The buyer was Ezeiza International Airport, which wanted it for its fire brigade. These experiences encouraged my son to set up a Peugeot auto repair shop (against our will) with a friend of his, who would later become this firm's representative in Argentina. Work and study do not always go hand in hand and so it was in this case. Carlos dropped his engineering studies and worked at his repair shop with great enthusiasm but low earnings.

My father's company grew astronomically when it began importing German-made ships into Argentina and other South American countries. Unfortunately, he also began to feel unwell – a flare-up of the condition he had developed during the war years – and he therefore asked my son for help. In response, Carlos sold his repair shop and went to work with his grandfather, which they eventually ran together. Sometime later, when my father was feeling stronger, they both traveled to Germany. Carlos was introduced to the managers of Thyssen and personally saw how work was conducted at company headquarters. It was my father's way of opening up business channels for his grandson in preparation for the day when he would be on his own. Once the business side of the trip was over, Carlos traveled across Europe by car and got as far as Venice, where, for the first time, he enjoyed the pleasures of youth. Until then, he had spent more time studying and working than having fun.

ARGENTINE CITIZENSHIP

Ever since we had arrived in Buenos Aires on March 1, 1943, I had been thinking about getting Argentine citizenship. At first, it was just a passing fancy that was immediately relegated to the background, not because I deemed it unimportant but because my mind was busy with other urgent matters that required all my attention. Back then, my main limitation had been the language barrier, which prevented me from communicating fluently, especially with salespeople and other ordinary folks. My time had also been taken up by the pleasant but not always easy task of caring for my children, my husband and my home. All my energy had been focused and spent on these responsibilities.

When our economic situation improved and my son started going to school, which left me a bit of free time, I began to research how to obtain Argentine citizenship. I was told I needed to produce documents proving my identity, but these were either still with Berta in Europe, or else did not exist. It thus became necessary to hire a lawyer to deal with the matter in a professional way. Yet, I wanted to do all the paperwork myself because I felt the effort would give me the right to be Argentine. I had already taken the first steps, but then I became pregnant with Lizy and her birth made me postpone these plans.

I felt defeated and dejected, but then, as usual, that inner strength swelled up inside of me – the same one that always pushed me forward – and I slowly began taking new steps towards the desired outcome, finding inspiration in that wise proverb that says, "If at first you don't succeed, try, try again." I asked questions, I explained my case, I collected information and I planned my next move. I had to interrupt my plans on several occasions, but after each effort something was always accomplished. The years went by, the children grew up, events followed their course, and by the time I got back to the citizenship issue, I was finally able to produce all the necessary documents without the help of any lawyer or agent. I was happy and proud of myself.

On November 11, 1962, at the National Civil and Commercial Court of First Instance No. 2 of the Federal Capital, five or six people took their oath before Judge Felipe Erlich Pratt, who granted them the much-desired Argentine citizenship. I was one of those people and I was very emotional. Dr. Erlich Pratt greeted and congratulated each of the brand-new Argentines and when he came to me, he asked as he hugged me warmly: "Why are you crying? Aren't you happy?" I replied that I was very moved because after so many years without a homeland, I had finally made my wish come true. From that moment on, every time someone asked me about my nationality, I could proudly and happily say "I am an Argentine!" I promised him that I would be a good citizen – and I have always tried to be one – as a tribute to everything that this country has given me. Ever since then, even though I am past the age of compulsory voting, every time there are elections I am only too happy to fulfill my duty as a citizen.

CARLOS' MARRIAGE

Soon after returning to Buenos Aires from his first trip to Europe, Carlos met Liliana Schiffs, his first wife and the mother of his three elder children: Cynthia, Pablo and Denise. Carlos and Liliana married on November 5, 1966 and they spent their wedding night at Carlos' small bachelor apartment. When they left for their honeymoon to Mar de Plata, Lizy and I went to lock up their apartment and found a letter addressed to me lying on a table. My son had written me a letter because he sensed a certain sadness in me now that he was married. We Jewish mothers tend to be very possessive of our children and when the first one gets married, we feel that the nest is starting to empty. This sadness does not always go unnoticed. The "Yiddishe Momme," the long-suffering, possessive mother with a special tenderness that is a combination of motherly instinct and devotion for her children, whom she pampers and cares for with passion and has a constant concern about their future, and with whom she is strict and rigorous when it comes to their schooling, is not an unknown figure either for Jews or for anyone else. I do not think of myself as a "Yiddishe Momme" (am I?!), but I confess that when Carlos got married and obviously left home, I suffered a little bit (just a little bit?!).

In the letter that my darling son wrote to me, he told me that his marriage would not change a thing in our mother-son relationship, and he thanked me for everything I had always done for him, stressing that he meant not the material things but all the great love and tenderness he had received from me. I always carried that letter with me, until one day in Madrid my purse was stolen and I lost it. But I remember it word for word and nobody can steal it away from my heart. It said:

> *Mom,*
> *I am writing this letter the day after my wedding, to thank you for everything you gave me all my life. God willing, I will one day be able to return at least part of the great affection you have shown me, and I am not talking about material things but about your motherly love, and even though I am now married nothing will change and we will continue to always be a mother and son who love each other.*
> *With all my love*
> *Carlos*

THE MIRAMAR HOUSE AND A SAD JOURNEY

In 1966 my father bought a house in Miramar that I still have and where I always spend my summers. He had probably been feeling unwell, because he said: "If I do not live, I want you to have this place so you can spend your holidays here." But we all made a joke of it and said he was just trying to be the center of attention, and that he wanted an excuse to pamper me. Certainly, he did not look ill at the time. He only spent a month in that house, because that year he returned to the capital early to prepare for a trip to Europe with my mother. They left on April 1, 1967 and were excited about the prospect of spending a restful time and going for walks in the countries they had first known in the glory of peace and then in the horror of war, and which were back in bloom again. Hundreds of memories and emotions awaited them there, as well as many new places to discover. Unfortunately, there were no friends or relatives waiting to greet them, as they had all either fled to other lands or died in the extermination camps or at the battlefronts. But beautiful Prague was there, as were the Sudetenland, Teplitz Schönau – my father's birthplace – the faraway Ölmutz, Vienna, the joie de vivre of Munich, the glitter of Paris and the greatness of Rome with its reddish buildings and its pine trees with tall, dark trunks and round, green tops.

Our thoughts were with them as they traveled across Europe, and we enjoyed hearing their reports when they telephoned. But on May 17, a call from my mother alarmed us to the point of desperation: They were at the Sacher Hotel in Vienna and my father was feeling very ill. I decided immediately to fly to Vienna and left the next day. The flight made a stopover in Rome and from there I called my parents and was able to talk to my father. He

Ilse's parents: Paul Hahn and his wife Karoline, née Goldschmidt.

reassured me by saying he felt fine again; that it was madness for me to be flying over, but that he liked the idea of seeing me. I told him I would be by his side in less than two hours and that he should take care of himself.

As soon as I made it through Austrian customs, I ran to a telephone booth to tell my parents I was on my way. This was the first time since March 5, 1938 – when I took the train to Ölmutz – that my father, mother and I were going to be together in Vienna, our hometown. Despite the anxiety I felt and the need to see for myself that my father was truly all right, I began to fantasize about us going to Grinzing[21] to drink the new wines and visiting our old home in the ninth district, and of course going to Vöslau to see our summer home, our dear Veilchen Villa. My mind was awhirl with memories, feelings and images from those far-off years when we had been so happy. But at the same time, a doubt formed in my mind: What would those places look like now? How many wounds did they sustain during the war, and how many more during Communism? How terrible would the scars be? Who was living there now?

THE WORST HAD ALREADY HAPPENED

I found a phone and my hands were shaking as I dialed the number of the Sacher Hotel. The operator who took my call put me through immediately. My mother picked up and when she heard my voice she started crying and repeating, "Papa is dead! Papa is dead!" It was dreadful. Even today, I still feel the same horrible sharp pain I felt at that moment. The wound still bleeds, as though I had just found out the terrible news.

I was unable to take the blow and I fainted. When I came to, there was an Argentine couple by my side to whom I had chatted on the flight. They were very kind and accompanied me to the hotel. But when I walked into the suite where my parents were staying, my pain was multiplied at the sight of the being I loved so much lying there dead. It was the first time I had ever seen a dead person, and the one lying there with his eyes open, appearing to look at his watch, was my father. It seemed as though he had spent the last minutes of his life in a battle against time – the time I had told him it would take me to get

21 Grinzing lies in the northwest of Vienna and is characterized by numerous forested ridges.

there from Rome. I do not remember much else. I know I was the one to shut his eyes. He had been dead only 20 minutes.

The first moments are always tough, but they are a lot tougher when you are in a hotel, far away from your loved ones. In such a situation, the relief of tears becomes a smothering impulse that you try to hold back out of consideration for the other people there. Once the first shock was over, I decided to call Buenos Aires to inform my children about the death of their grandfather. I was unable to say “Grandpa is dead,” and instead just barely managed to say “Grandpa is no longer with us.” A long time later my children told me that they went into their study room and cried sad, desperate, bitter tears for a long time, hugging each other in their grief and incapable of uttering anything other than “O papa! O papa!”

My father died in the afternoon of Friday, May 19, 1967. By the time we managed to get in touch with the Jewish congregation of Vienna, which would take care of his remains, the first star was already out and *Shabbat* had begun – the holy day for Jews, when they must observe a very rigid liturgy that includes a ban on burials and other funeral rites. This meant that the funeral could only take place on Sunday; meanwhile, the hotel management informed us that, because of in-house rules, the body had to be removed immediately. So with great distress we had to accept having my father taken out of the hotel at midnight and driven to the morgue – there was no other option.

The next day, Carlos boarded a KLM plane from Buenos Aires to Amsterdam, then took a connecting flight to Vienna, where he arrived on Sunday afternoon. I was able to wait for him on the tarmac after airport authorities granted me special permission, given my circumstances. The meeting with Carlos consisted of one long hug, many tears and very few words. Grief kept us nearly silent until we reached the hotel, but that night we began remembering the good and the sad times in my father’s life; the lessons he had taught us; his affectionate and protective attitude towards us. We looked like two children whom the death of their father had turned into sad, disconcerted little orphans.

During his last living moments, my father had expressed a wish to “return to Buenos Aires.” There is a family sepulcher in Vienna that lies nearly empty, because the gas chambers of the extermination camps reduced the bodies of our loved ones to ashes that were impossible to recover. My father could have been buried there, but following his instructions to my mother, we arranged to have his remains flown to Buenos Aires, the city that he loved so much and to which he felt so grateful; the place that had taken him and my mother in when they had arrived from Europe as two poor, lonely immigrants who spoke no Spanish.

Carlos made an effort to overcome his own grief and handle all the necessary paperwork to have his grandfather's remains flown to Argentina – a sad undertaking in any situation, but even more painful when the remains are those of a loved one. Carlos was relieved to find that a good friend and former schoolmate worked at the Argentine Consulate in Vienna. This friend knew how much Carlos had loved his grandfather and immediately began helping him in such an efficient way that ten days later the coffin was already in Amsterdam and ready for transportation to Buenos Aires on KLM, the Dutch airline that had awarded my father a "Flying Dutchman" card years before because he had been such a frequent flyer.

While the casket was being transported to Argentina, my mother, son and I traveled to Switzerland, where my mother stayed with a friend while Carlos and I continued to Dusseldorf, Germany – a country that was still clearly in mourning over the recent death of its former Chancellor Konrad Adenauer – to inform the Thyssen managers about the death of their representative in Argentina. We returned to Switzerland to pick up my mother and all three of us flew to Buenos Aires on Monday, June 5, where my husband, daughter and many friends were waiting for us. On Thursday, June 8, the coffin containing my father's remains arrived on the same KLM plane he had sat on so many times on his way to Europe.

The funeral took place the next day at Liniers cemetery at Lizy's initiative, since she felt that "as Grandpa had lived, so should he take his final resting." We paid a significant sum of money for the privilege of having him buried there, and part of what we paid to the ÁMIA – the Jewish Association in Argentina – was donated to an Israeli charity.

OVERCOMING GRIEF AND MOVING ON

It was very hard to overcome my father's death. It took us a long time and required great personal effort. Filling the void he had left behind meant taking over all the responsibilities he had dealt with. We had always felt secure in the knowledge that his fortitude, intelligence and sharp wit would solve any troublesome situation that came our way, allowing the rest of us to lead carefree lives and not feel weighed down by problems.

Carlos continued to work in my father's office but soon after, Thyssen appointed a new representative in Buenos Aires. As for Lizy, she felt the loss of her grandfather very deeply, not only because she had loved him dearly, but also because she was very young and sensitive when he died. We thought she should get away from the spirit of sadness that pervaded our home; we wanted her to enjoy her youth without our casting of shadows over it. Therefore, we decided to send her to the United States, to take an orientation course at Ohio University, where some relatives of my husband were teaching. After spending a month in Ohio, she went to London and stayed with my cousin Robert Elias – the son of Gertrude Elias, née Hahn, who was my father's sister and had died of cancer three days after Nazi troops occupied Vienna. He is my only remaining blood relative.

Lizy spent several happy months with him, his wife and their two children. The bonds they developed are still strong and they frequently meet in London or Madrid, where Lizy now lives. Later, my daughter went to the Sorbonne in Paris to study French while she worked as an au pair for a family there, caring for the children twice a week in exchange for a room in the attic. She spent six months in Paris, during which time we wired her the money she needed for her expenses. But she had made up her mind that she was going to make it on her own, and wanted to feel independent and self-sufficient. She made her own decisions, earned her own money, learned languages or perfected the ones she already knew, and built up a group of friends. In Paris she was witness to the famous events of May 1968 – I can imagine her with her great blue eyes open wide so as not to miss a thing – and she led a Bohemian life that she adored and which she handled in a balanced and mature way. Lizy had grown up.

Later she went to Israel with some American friends, then Greece, and finally spent a wonderful year in Europe. A year later she returned to Buenos Aires. She was the same affectionate daughter and sister, but her character was stronger and she was admirably sure of herself. She had become the person I wanted her to be: a free, purposeful and successful young woman.

We went to Brazil together and I spent a week enjoying her company after such a long absence. I wanted to be alone with her, without friends or family to take her away from me. I could sense that from now on I would be with my daughter, but no longer with my little girl – she was now a woman through and through. We returned to Buenos Aires at the end of August 1968, after enjoying our "mother-daughter" time together, and were greeted with sad news: A first cousin of my father's, Franz Joseph Hahn, whom we loved dearly, was dying. He knew the end was near and kept saying he wanted to see me and talk to me to relieve the pain he felt in his soul and give me his blessing. He was able to have his wish fulfilled, and it felt good to hear him out and receive his blessing. He died at two in the morning, surrounded by his loved ones, and leaving us with a sweet memory that cushioned the blow of his death. God granted him a peaceful death.

A SERIOUS HEALTH PROBLEM

In early September, I began feeling sharp stomach pains. The first doctor I saw said it was my body's way of externalizing the grief I felt over the death of Joseph Hahn. But the pain kept getting worse, so we went to see another practitioner, Dr. Malamud, who diagnosed peritonitis and said I needed surgery right away. The operation lasted seven hours, during which time the damage to the peritoneum was fixed and a tumor, which I had no idea was there in the first place, was extracted and sent for immediate pathology. My overall state of health was alarming. Such a long operation under general anesthesia, plus an examination to ensure the tumor had not spread, had wrought havoc on my body. When the surgeon reported that he could not guarantee I would survive, because he suspected the tumor was malignant, my husband had a heart attack, Lizy fainted and Carlos stormed out of the sanatorium in confused despair, not knowing where he was going or why.

After more than 20 days in hospital and putting up with blood transfusions, probes, respirators and other devices aimed at relieving patients' suffering – even if it feels like torture – I returned home, still too weak to stand. When I got there, I learned that the reason my husband had not visited me at the hospital was not because he had had flu, as I had been led to believe, but because he was recovering from a heart attack that nobody had told me about. Slowly we both recovered and because I am one of those people with a "precarious health of steel," two months later I was able to invite the doctors who treated me to my own birthday party, to celebrate my "rebirth." The surgeon who had operated on me said that the survival rate of people with similar symptoms was "one in a million." Once again, I felt certain that I was under God's protection.

LIFE GOES ON

Once this series of sad events was over – the biggest one being my father's death in Vienna and having his remains flown over – a period of bonanza followed. The time had come to reorganize and surround ourselves with happy things. Still, not everything was rosy.

Lizy completed her sociology studies at Buenos Aires University. She had always been a brilliant student since she had promised me as a young girl that she would rise from the bottom to the top of the class. She graduated with honors, filling us with pride and happiness. Later, she went to a university summer camp and met a young man whom she fell hopelessly in love with. We were unable to persuade her to spend a little more time on her own, or that we thought she was still too young to make formal commitments. Such is love — stronger than good sense and reason. Soon after that, she told us she wanted to try living on her own and rented a two-room apartment. She was working with her father, earning money and maintaining her self-reliant attitude. Then one day she said she wanted to get married, and I must confess I again felt like a "Yiddishe Momme" who suffers when the young ones leave the nest. Lizy and Alberto Swiec were married on December 22, 1975. My husband and I gave them a furnished apartment as a wedding gift, and Carlos gave them a new car. She was very happy.

Not long afterwards, they decided to live in a different country, since they could not see a bright future for themselves in Argentina. It was 1976 and dark times loomed under the clear southern skies. They left. The goodbyes were painful. We would be separated by thousands of kilometers, and we had to accept that. First they spent a few months in Israel, then moved to Barcelona, Spain, where things were very tough at first. Lizy, who has always been a fighter, had no qualms about taking a job as a cashier at a supermarket while she continued to study. I did not know about her financial troubles because Carlos was secretly sending her money during that time.

MY SECOND GREAT LOSS

Towards the middle of the year, Lizy announced that she and her husband would be coming to Buenos Aires during their summer break. My husband and I awaited their arrival anxiously. I began rearranging things around the house to make it look beautiful, and was so caught up in my cleaning that two nights before Lizy and Alberto's arrival I turned down my husband's offer to go to the movies together – I wanted to finish what I was doing – so he went alone. Around 30 minutes later I was startled by the sound of the phone ringing. An unfamiliar voice asked me very quietly: "Are you Mrs. Kaufmann?" "Yes, I am," I replied in a puzzled tone, not knowing whether it was a good idea to confirm my identity. "Are you alone?" the voice continued. "What's going on? Who are you?" I asked without answering the question, while an odd, upsetting feeling came over me. "Is there a family member nearby?" "No, not here, but I can call my son. Who are you? Could you please tell me what's going on?" "Mrs. Kaufmann, your husband is not well. He had an attack outside the movie theater. Please give me your son's telephone number. I am calling from police station number 17."

I gave him Carlos' number without thinking, hung up and called our doctor to ask him to go down to the station to check if my husband was indeed there and to assist him. Almost immediately after hanging up, I received a call from Carlos. "I'm coming over to pick you up," he said, without any further explanations. No more words were necessary to know that something bad had happened and that this bad thing could not be fixed. I asked Carlos directly whether his father was dead, but he did not reply, which spoke for itself. When we got to the police station our doctor was already there and he confirmed my worst fears. "Mrs. Kaufmann, I am sorry to tell you that your husband is dead." Once again, as though touched by an accursed fate, a loved one had died abruptly. Was it my destiny to lose the people I loved this way? When I came to, I was in Carlos' arms and we were both crying. "We have to tell Lizy. She must still be in Barcelona," was all I managed to say.

We kept vigil over my husband at home. I wanted him to spend the last night in our house. I know there were a lot of people who came in and out, offering their condolences and talking to us. I have vague, overlapping memories of both familiar and unfamiliar faces going by, my hand being held, getting hugged and hearing words of sympathy. I remember that I waited for Lizy's arrival with great anxiety, but it was a different kind of anxiety than the one my husband and I had felt just a few hours earlier. This one was bitter, upsetting and filled with loneliness.

The impact of my husband's death had thrown me into a state of confusion and my mind was awhirl with the memories of our years in Prague during the Nazi occupation, with all its bitter, unforgettable events: the danger, the massacres, the persecution, the paralyzing fear and the astuteness and audacity we had had to display to save ourselves. I saw images of the Hotel Flora, of the secret meetings to listen to the BBC on the radio, of the morning of our wedding, of the SS officials knocking the heels of their hard boots together, of the shrapnel tearing patriots to pieces in revenge for the death of Heydrich, of the train ride to Dresden, Paris and Bilbao, of the *Cabo de Buena Esperanza*, of our arrival in Argentina with five dollars in our pockets, of the first years of hardship and struggle to make ends meet. I remembered the piano chords that my husband Bela, who loved music so much, used to play later when we were prosperous. I thought of my family growing up and getting stronger during the boom years. I did not call these images to mind; they came to me of their own accord, as if telling me: "Look, all of this is yours and his. This is your life, the life you lived by his side."

In the middle of so much turmoil and despair, of so much pain and confusion, I had the feeling – I would even say the certainty – that this life full of risk and hardship caused first by the war and its consequences, and then by our own efforts to prosper, comprised an enormous heritage that belonged exclusively to the two of us. It was a heritage that was indivisible, indestructible and untransferable, and which could not be bequeathed to anyone because it was impossible for anyone to inherit it. It is hard to believe that such a huge collection of mostly negative and painful events can make for such an important, solid, consistent and unforgettable personal legacy.

My daughter and her husband, who were flying in from Barcelona, arrived at the cemetery just as the coffin was being lowered into its grave. Lizy's grief and pain were indescribable. She could not resign herself to the fact that her father was gone and neither Carlos nor I had the strength to comfort her. It was June 1976. Bela died on Tuesday the twenty-second.

AFTERWARDS

We were ravaged by shock and pain. It felt good to have Lizy near me, but seeing her so sad weighed heavily upon me. Carlos immediately took up his father's business responsibilities without neglecting his own, which were already bringing him significant revenues. His intelligence and capacity for hard work were sorely tested during this time, but he managed to handle everything with help from Lizy, who stayed in Buenos Aires for six months and took over the helm of the company. Thereafter, Lizy and her husband returned to Spain. She took up her studies again and eventually obtained a position at the university, where she slowly but surely began climbing the rungs of academia. Always a hard worker, she did not drop out and instead graduated in sociology in Madrid. Later, she went to Paris to get her PhD at the Sorbonne. To all this effort, she later added the birth of her first child, a beautiful baby she named Alex, on May 13, 1980.

I went to Barcelona for the delivery and spent six weeks helping Lizy and enjoying the delightful task of caring for my daughter's first son – a truly unforgettable experience for me. Alex is now a handsome young man; he is earnest, dependable, affectionate and very protective of his mother and sister Andrea, who is six years younger than he is. Andrea was born in Madrid on November 8, 1986 and is now a refined and charming young woman who speaks with a delicious Madrid accent. She is intelligent and a good student; she loves animals, especially horses, and is an expert rider.

After my husband's death, Carlos suggested that I take over Bela's company, since his own affairs were taking up an increasing amount of time and effort. He appointed a few trusted aides to show me the ropes and help me with

Ilse in Spain with her grandchildren, Andrea and Alex.

my tasks, excusing himself for not training me personally and explaining that his own business was growing by the day and required all of his precious time. I quickly and easily learned how to handle the company my husband had created. Besides, it was very interesting: The firm imported microscopes, theodolites, anti-hail rockets for use in agriculture and other optics-based devices. I traveled to Hungary, France, Germany and most of Argentina. I attended trade fairs and exhibitions and dealt with many clients from around the world.

Working did me the world of good and I was soon rewarded with success. It made me feel useful, important and respected. My presence was required at major firms in many parts of the world and my work quickly yielded good returns. Then my son recommended that I move to a different house, since, in his opinion, I should not continue living in the same apartment where we had kept vigil over his father. Fortunately, I was able to find a suitable apartment and I have lived there ever since. Because it was still under construction when I bought it, I had it built according to my own tastes, and the money I was making allowed me to furnish and decorate it the way I liked. I have been very comfortable there – enjoying the terrace full of plants in bloom almost year-round and admiring the views of the botanical garden, where the setting sun lights up the tops of the trees.

This spacious, comfortable apartment was the first home of my very own after so many years of moving around during the war, when we were constantly running away from persecution and danger, searching for a security we never found and effectively becoming urban nomads who hung on to a dwindling amount of increasingly worn-out belongings.

CARLOS' DIVORCE AND REMARRIAGE

In 1982 my son Carlos and his wife Liliana got divorced. They had married very young – Carlos was even younger than she was – and from the very beginning they had run up against serious family opposition, which had manifested itself in ways that had been difficult for them to accept. Among other things, my father had not gone to their wedding. However, it was Liliana who was there by Carlos' side during our family's growth years, when we strove to build our assets through trial and error and constant daily efforts that wore everyone out. She was there for support in the midst of the economic whirlwind that laid the foundations for their own later wealth until, pulled under by the weight of prosperity, they became isolated from each other and drew further and further apart until the separation was complete. They had three children: Cynthia was born on August 25, 1969; Pablo on February 3, 1971; and Denise on June 8, 1972. As is always the case in such circumstances, the family was shaken up by the divorce and everyone's habits changed. With family unity disintegrated by the separation, each member began experimenting with new lifestyles that were appropriate in some cases but not in others. This led, in turn, to a search for new solutions that were often anything but that.

So they became nomads, too; but they were spiritual and emotional nomads. In their confusion they sought out landscapes filled with alluring mirages and nonexistent oases. But these evanescent dreams could not quench their thirst for the order, the warmth and the sense of belonging that their family had once provided. Carlos rented an apartment in the Belgrano area and moved in alone. I tried to help him with the domestic chores and often went over to his place when he was not there. He came to my house relatively often, sometimes with his children, who were living with their mother. The goal of these family visits was to put my mind at ease, as he could see that I was very worried.

His eldest child, Cynthia, practically moved in with me. She came over almost every day, especially on Friday afternoons, and stayed until Monday morning when she had to go to school. She came and went, met her friends or went shopping, but she was mostly at my apartment. I fixed her lunch and always made sure I packed it in a way that would be spill-proof and easy to carry. I enjoyed making her breakfast and dinner and preparing her bed when she wanted to go to sleep. In my eyes and in my heart, she symbolized the family, my family, whose members had gone their different ways through the natural course of events, leaving me alone. So I pampered her and gave her my "Yiddishe Bubbe" love, and she made me happy. I have very sweet memories of that period when Cynthia spent so much time with me, lighting up the apartment with her presence, her affection and her youth.

Carlos continued to make progress at work and had by now amassed a fortune that afforded him a very comfortable life. I was also making good progress at my deceased husband's firm and was earning a good salary. These years were marked by a dynamic of growing prosperity that proved the truth of the saying: "Money does not make happiness, but it sure helps it along." The things that had gotten out of hand when my son got divorced were now back on track.

Sometime later, Carlos remarried and this time his wife was considerably younger than he was. She was an ambitious woman, divorced and without children, who dazzled Carlos with her poise, her sharp intelligence and her special training. A lawyer by trade, she was a member of the Jewish-Argentine elite and her professional and social circles were different from those of Carlos, who moved in the world of local and European business.

My son's first wife, Liliana, eventually rebuilt her own life, married a very pleasant and refined man of Italian origin, and moved to Rome with him. Carlos' children moved back in with him and easily accepted Claudia, his new wife, as a new member of the family. They had a good life that was sustained financially by Carlos' business acumen and socially by Claudia's natural *savoir faire*. They spent their weekends at a country club in the north of Greater Buenos Aires, played sports, had active social lives and traveled often.

AN ANEURYSM

When Carlos and Claudia went on trips together, I took care of my grandchildren in their absence whenever they needed me. When Carlos planned a trip to Israel with Claudia, he asked me to go with them, which made me very happy because I had always wanted to see the Promised Land. However, before our departure Carlos suddenly started feeling sick. He was dizzy, had intense vomiting spells and rapidly began losing his eyesight. We rushed him to the hospital and soon found out that he had a brain aneurysm and had to undergo emergency surgery. The operation was a success and by the time he was moved to the recovery room, the sharp pains that had made him suffer so intensely for hours were gone. It was a miracle that he did not die. It was, once again, God's protection manifesting itself.

Carlos recovered in just a few months and we later took that trip to Israel, although first I went to Spain to see Lizy, then to Switzerland and then met up with Carlos and his wife, where he and I wanted to express our gratitude for his miraculous recovery at the Western Wall in Jerusalem. That was where my new daughter-in-law told me that she was pregnant. On November

22, 1985, my grandson Nicolás was born in Buenos Aires, and Carlos was especially loving and protective of this late child of his, perhaps because he seemed so small compared to his other teenage kids. He took Nicolás everywhere with him, which meant always traveling with an elaborate setup consisting of a nanny, baby clothes, crib, stroller, bathtub and other necessary items for the child's comfort.

Everything around Carlos and his family had progressively turned into a flurry of activity that kept slowly but surely accelerating. There were more and more trips, an intense social life that placed great demands on everyone, successful and exciting business dealings, the children's difficult teenage years, the progress made by the baby, who was already crawling, then walking, then talking; there was Claudia following the latest fashion trends and directing this peaceful little army, raising her own child and coming and going every day – they were all trapped in a whirlwind that threatened to devour them without their noticing it, caught up as they were in this happiness of sorts.

CARLOS' DEATH

There they were, happy and busy with all sorts of endeavors and schedules, when suddenly Carlos felt sick again and had to be urgently hospitalized at Hospital Alemán once more. When I heard the news that morning, my grandson Pablo was just saying goodbye because the next day he was leaving on his graduation trip. Our joy for his trip quickly turned into serious concern for Carlos' health. That afternoon the doctors said he needed surgery and the operation took place that same night. Afterwards, he was admitted to the intensive care ward, where access to patients is limited to two short daily visits, one mid-morning and the other in the evening – no doubt as a barrier to emotions.

I was naturally very concerned. I could feel myself growing more anxious and disconcerted by the minute. A great weight settled on my shoulders, while at the same time a kind of paralysis crept over my arms and legs, making them go numb. Everyone tried to soothe me, saying this was just a preventive measure, that he would be well taken care of, and that being there would help him get better quickly. I was making a great effort to control my own uneasiness, but I have to confess that my mouth was completely dry and my throat, constricted by intense strain, barely allowed me to speak. I tried to convince myself that the treatment would work, thinking how only last Sunday, August 7, had been Children's Day, and how Carlos had taken his kids to a toy store to let them pick out a present. Later, I had been at their house to celebrate the day together. Everything had been so normal and Carlos seemed to be fine and happy. Yes, I had to calm down and stop seeing ghosts.

At lunchtime, everyone left to have something to eat. I remained alone in the hallway next to the intensive care ward. I needed to be near my son and could not leave him alone. Had I not always been there by his side ever since September 10, 1941, when he was born in Prague in the middle of the Nazi danger, even as I lay discriminated against in a delivery room that was "for Jewish women only"? And even before that, had I not stood up to my father when he called me thoughtless after learning that I was pregnant, and had I not made the decision to defend the life beating inside me? So even if I could not go inside the ward and hold his hand or stroke his forehead, how could I leave my son alone? I felt I had to be as near to him as possible, as if my nearness could give him the necessary strength to defeat the illness that kept him in bed; as if by being out there I might feel his heart beating or hear his breathing. And there I stayed, as close to him as I could, as if his hand were holding mine, as if I could kiss his burning forehead, as if my mere presence could cure him and save him. But it was all in vain and it was devastating. At 1.30 in the afternoon on Thursday, August 11, 1988, Carlos passed away.

Death, that enemy that had hounded me so often, threatening to take me or my loved ones away; that enemy that I had so often managed to fool during the war, although it had snuffed out the lives of almost my entire family in the extermination ovens; this death was not content with the high price that had already been paid. Now it was also taking my son, a young man who was beginning to enjoy the prosperity he had achieved through his own intelligence and hard work. He was leaving behind a wife and kids – some were barely teenagers and others mere children – who were struck by the unexpectedness of his death and ravaged by the pain of it.

In the middle of this desolate landscape I could picture the face of my daughter, who loved her brother so much, flooding with tears upon learning of his death. I would have to break the sorrowful news to Lizy, who was traveling in the United States with her husband and children. But how could I tell her that her brother was dead? Where would I find the strength to phone her?

While I asked myself these terrible questions, what little resolve I had left abandoned me completely and I felt myself dying too. I experienced the most heartrending pain and the most tremendous bitterness, even as the hand of anguish clenched my throat, preventing me from screaming my son's name to the four winds and calling out to him so I might hold him back and wrest him out of the sharp claws of death. But this time death was victorious and took him away forever, ripping my soul apart.

Nearly 14 years have passed since that day, yet I still feel the same stifled cry inside my throat. The death of a child is the greatest pain a human being can suffer. Every time I pronounce his name I feel myself splitting in two and one part of me goes with him.

I told Lizy and she and her husband arrived just in time for the burial. I was standing all alone at the cemetery, since Claudia and Carlos' three older children had formed a tight little group some distance away. When the ceremony was over, seeing me so hurt and alone, the rabbi came up to me and asked: "Who are you, Madam?" And when I replied: "I am Carlos' mother," I suddenly became fully aware of the true extent of my loneliness, and felt completely abandoned. Thankfully, Lizy showed up at that precise moment and her embrace, in the middle of the tears and the pain, brought some solace to my ravaged soul. Lizy was unable to say goodbye to her beloved brother, just like years earlier she had not been able to say goodbye to her father or her grandfather. They were three trying tests for my dear daughter and ever since then we have always been there for each other and feel more united than ever before.

From the cemetery we all drove to Carlos' house, but once we got there, Claudia, her sister, father, mother and Carlos' business partner locked themselves up inside my son's office to talk, while Lizy, her husband and I were left standing alone in the living room, feeling perplexed. While we could not understand the reason for this odd, inconsiderate attitude, we thought we understood the message behind it: There was nothing more for us to do there; our presence was no longer necessary. And so, crushed by the tremendous sorrow of losing Carlos and the additional grief of the scene that had just taken place, we left the house that had been my son's and which, now that he was gone, seemed to have found new owners already. It was as though one tragic chapter had ended and another one had begun – one that was saddening, unexpected, inexplicable and unwonted, and which has lasted 14 years already. I do not know when this chapter will truly end.

For several days I was paralyzed by grief. I was unable to walk – I had lost my balance – and I think I was unable to talk as well. I could hardly see and was barely aware of what was going on around me. Later, we had to tell my mother that Carlos was dead and this thankless task fell to Lizy, two of our friends, my doctor and I. My mother was 92 years old at the time and her reaction was typical of very elderly people when they sustain a great loss: She displayed an unexpected resignation that was somewhat disconcerting – perhaps because of the proximity to her own death.

A few days later, Cynthia came to my house and knelt by my bed. She was very sad, but just as sweet and affectionate as ever. She sat there for some time without speaking, and then said: "Grandma, I always dreamed that on my wedding day, when I walked into the temple, I would be holding my father's arm. Now that he isn't here anymore, I am asking you to always be with me, because you are the only part of him I have left."

Later, odd things happened. Claudia and the children became very distant and we found out that a tombstone had been placed over Carlos' grave that did not have my or Lizy's name on it. My daughter, however, later had our names engraved into the marble. Eventually, Claudia and Carlos' children moved to the United States and we never heard from them again. The kids

Lizy and Carlos with Lizy's son, Alex, 1980.

grew up, went to college and graduated. During all that time, I had neither news from my grandchildren, nor the consolation of a photograph or a phone call. It has been a long and sad 14-year wait full of dashed hopes, but I still dream of seeing them again one day.[22]

LIFE SINCE THEN

Meanwhile, my mother was ageing fast and when she turned 98 she came to live with me, since at that point she could no longer take care of herself. It was a big sacrifice for me, because by then I was used to living alone – but it had to be done and I fulfilled my duties as a daughter, even if it was hard watching her gradually deteriorate and trying to come to terms with it. All her life she had been a princess who had had to be waited on, pampered and escorted at all times, and so she was until the day she died in my apartment, on September 4, 1994.

When I was released from the responsibility of caring for my mother, I traveled to Spain to visit my daughter and her children. Lizy, who has been divorced for some years now, has done an admirable job with her kids. When I got to Madrid, I found two beautiful teenagers who were kind, intelligent people. My daughter's efforts and dedication are bearing fruit. I am proud of my grandchildren and even more so of my daughter, who has been able to provide proper guidance and education. All four of us have a strong spiritual connection; we talk frequently and recently they came to Buenos Aires to see me.

After talking it over with Lizy, I decided to stay in my pretty apartment across from the botanical garden in Buenos Aires, because Madrid's weather is too intense for me. Besides, I am fascinated by the southern skies. Also, Argentina has been my homeland for many years now and I love this country that gave me everything when I arrived with nothing more than the equivalent of five of today's dollars. Lizy, on the other hand, decided to stay in Madrid because she has a good career there and, most importantly, because Spain is her children's homeland. Their father also lives there and they are very close.

22 Editor's note: Years later, when Ilse had already moved to Alcalá, Cynthia came with her husband and brought her son Lucas to finally meet his great grandmother.

And so life went on in Buenos Aires, where I spent most of my time thinking about the old days, about the dearly departed, and looking at old photographs that Berta was kind enough to keep for years and which she later sent me. These images helped me relive the golden days of my childhood and adolescence, and also the sinister years under the Nazis. I also thought about my time in Argentina, where I raised my children in peace while we worked to rebuild the happy, easy life we had lost when war broke out.

For a long time I had been writing down dates and events in a notebook, thus recording my reminiscences in a kind of chronicle or memory aid. My intention was to perhaps one day write the story of my life, as a legacy to my grandchildren and as one more testimony of what life was like for European Jews during World War II. This was a difficult goal for me, since I am not fluent in Spanish, but since so many things in my life have seemed unattainable yet eventually came true, I never dropped this project altogether. I didn't know how it would be done, but felt it would somehow happen.

MY WISH COMES TRUE

They say that if you wish for something very intensely, it finally comes true. So one day, something happened that put my dream on the right track to become a reality. My daughter Lizy traveled from Spain to Canada, where she stayed with an old friend, Ruth Schweitzer, who runs an art gallery. At the time, the gallery was showing work by an Argentine painter and printmaker and Lizy liked her work so much that she bought some pieces and took them home to Madrid. Soon after, she came to Argentina and the first thing she asked me to do was to find this artist so she could talk to her. We found her name, Mirta Kupferminc, in the phone book.

However, Mirta no longer lived at that address. Fortunately, the person who picked up the phone gave us the number of her workshop, where we were finally able to reach her. Lizy went over to meet Mirta and to see her work, and she was fascinated. She quickly set up an appointment so I, too, could meet this woman and get to know her wonderful art. I immediately accepted, intrigued by Lizy's stories about her. The next day, I went over to the workshop and met Mirta, who introduced us to her sister Marga. We quickly became friends and they both decided to call their mother, Mrs.

Agie Kupferminc, who joined us. Agie and I soon discovered that we had war memories in common. She had gone through the tremendous experience of being deported to the concentration camp at Auschwitz, where she was a prisoner until the end of the war. Our testimonies, which were captured on video by a journalist working in Steven Spielberg's research team, are already part of the archives at the United States Holocaust Memorial Museum.

It was while we were both briefly telling each other about our experiences that I expressed my wish to find someone to write the story of my life, since my Spanish was not good enough to do it myself. When she heard this, Marga said in a very firm tone: "I know the person who can write your story," and she gave me a name and telephone number, adding that this woman was a great friend of hers. Marga Kupferminc's generosity got my book project started and I will be eternally grateful to her.

The next day, I dialed the number and spoke with Helena Pardo, who was already expecting my call. We set up an appointment to meet and to discuss the project and on Tuesday, September 1, 1998, at three in the afternoon, Helena knocked on my door. We had a formal but very cordial conversation that served as a mutual introduction; I summarized my life story for her and handed her some of the notes I had taken over the years to help refresh my memory, as well as some cassette recordings. Helena listened to my story, looked at the photographs and the supporting documents and said she would write my biography.

We began meeting once a week at my apartment, where I gave her details about the various episodes of my life. She took notes and recorded our conversations so she could later give the ideas literary form. Our meetings soon became a pleasant routine during which she read out loud the paragraphs she had written since our last encounter, and which I corrected or approved. I would then continue evoking memories from the past, some of which were kept in remote recesses of my brain. She recorded this as well and took more notes, then went home to her computer to produce a few more paragraphs.

Part of the pleasure of this routine was having our five o'clock tea, which consisted of Harrogate's decaffeinated tea brought from London by Lizy and croissants from Canela or Big Mamma, two pastry shops in Palermo, the area where we both live – no more than 500 meters apart from each other. Needless to say, from the moment we met we became great friends and this friendship has extended to her family, as well as to Lizy and her children.

Putting this book together has been a wonderful experience, because it has made me relive all the emotions of the past – the great and the small, the sweet and the bitter. During this time, I have cried, laughed and lived my life over again – a life that was not forgotten but which by now seemed a bit distant, a bit faded, though always present in my heart. Remembering all of these events in the course of a conversation, safe in the knowledge that the person sitting across from me was listening with her heart, made the memories flow clear and true, with a comforting freshness that made me better understand my own life, my attitudes and those of other people, and the true depth of my affections.

The emotional catharsis reflected in this written chronicle of my life has also touched my daughter Lizy, who recently told me that parts of the story made her understand many things that she had previously been unable to comprehend or accept. My grandchildren Alex and Andrea, who were the inspiration for this book, also read a few passages in a sort of "family-only premiere" prior to publication and they said they were happy to learn about their family's roots. As for me, I must confess that it is only now, after talking to Helena and re-reading my own story, that I begin to have a deep understanding of who Edith Ilse Kaufmann, née Hahn, truly is.

I must also stress that Helena was never the kind of interviewer who pried into my affairs in search of sensationalist details. From the outset, she became part of the story, someone who inspired trust and made me feel understood, and who helped bring the memories to the surface even when they were in the deepest recesses of my mind. I am sure that she suffered greatly when she wrote the gloomier passages about the war, that she felt the same horrible fear we did, and that she was relieved every time we managed to overcome a dangerous situation. She experienced everything that I was reliving as I talked to her, and she did so with sincerity, affection and great respect. Helena and I decided we would be the coauthors of this book, although she always says that this is *my* book, to which I always reply that no, this is *her* book. Fortunately, I think I have hit upon the right formula to describe it: *This is my life, but it is her book.*

It was wonderful to see my dream come true and be able to leave my grandchildren this testimony about their roots. This book is dedicated to *all of them*, and to the revered memory of my son Carlos, to my daughter Lizy, to the memory of my parents and of my good husband Bela, and as a tribute to all the people – those of my own blood and the others as well – who were the victims of the greatest and cruelest madness of all time, which I have described in this story as "the darkest night in the history of humankind": the Holocaust.

Ilse, Buenos Aires, 2002.

EPILOGUE

August 28, 2009

Ilse's voice has gone quiet forever. She passed away on March 26, 2006, at six o'clock in the morning, just as the sun was beginning to rise in the Madrid sky. She died after two weeks in hospital, where she fought her last battle. In these last few pages, I provide a brief account of what Ilse did during the final months of her stay in Argentina and her return to Europe. Going back was not something that had seemed to be in her plans, and for those of us who loved her and wanted her to stay in Buenos Aires, it was a very hard decision to accept.

I AM STARTING TO REMEMBER

By late June 2000, I had already finished the book about Ilse's life. She was turning 80 on November 7 of that year, and her daughter Alicia – Lizy – was to fly to Buenos Aires from Madrid for the birthday party. I helped Ilse select the catering service, since she liked to organize things well in advance and was anxious not to leave everything until the last minute. I was a witness to her enthusiasm, her teenage excitement and, with her usual trademark elegance, her desire to offer her guests all the best. Her efforts were rewarded: The birthday party was a refined, happy, heartwarming affair. Ilse received not just warm wishes and words of praise from her friends – Alicia

Ilse's eightieth birthday, November 2000, Buenos Aires. **From left:** Liliana Fiorin (Carlos' first wife), Alicia (Lizy), Ilse, Diana Weisberg (Alicia's best friend), Helena Pardo (behind), Agie Kupferminc.

had asked Ilse's friends, months in advance, to put down in writing what she meant to them – but also beautiful presents and many, many flowers. She was ecstatic, as flowers were her passion.

ILSE'S SOLITUDE

After Ilse and I completed our joint task of reconstructing Ilse's life, which we did at weekly Thursday meetings, there was no reason for us to stop seeing each other or for our friendship to get any weaker. We talked on the phone several times a day. She was a very good conversationalist and could talk about a wide range of topics. She always kept abreast of developments through television and the news magazines that she collected, and she loved to tell me about breaking stories and discuss them with me. She used to watch the international TV broadcaster *Deutsche Welle* and was a regular reader of *La Nación* and *Argentinisches Tageblatt*. She also spoke to Alicia several times a week who, besides bringing her up to speed with family news, also shared all kinds of news stories coming out of Europe, whether political, economic, scientific or other. This, combined with her sporadic contact with her remaining friends who, at this stage in life, were passing away with some regularity, was the soul food that kept her going.

Nevertheless, weekends were difficult for Ilse. Her maid was off duty from four o'clock on Saturday afternoon until seven o'clock on Monday morning, and Ilse got depressed being home alone, especially on those long weekends that sometimes stretched from Friday to Tuesday, thanks to the government's decision to shuffle around the "corralito" bank holidays in order to encourage tourism. I did not always have the time to ask her out or spend time with her, as my own family and social obligations often took up the entire time afforded by those days off. Sometimes, in her solitude, she would complain that she did not feel well, and it was disturbing to know that all she really needed was some company, which I could not give her. Nevertheless, Ivonne Pittaluga, whom Ilse treated as though she were one of her own grandchildren, often spent time with her. The Pittalugas had become her adopted family in Argentina; they had been neighbors ever since Ilse and her family arrived in Buenos Aires, and she loved them dearly.

On the occasional weekend, Ilse and I would have tea at one of the cafés on Avenida del Libertador, or else Juan and I would take her out to lunch at one of her favorite restaurants. Alicia came to Buenos Aires as often as she could, but her travel options were limited as she had to care for her young children – Andrea was still a teenager – and she also had academic and professional obligations. When Alicia was in Madrid, Ilse would call me up, find something for us to do together, and give me advice as though I were her own daughter. ("Be careful, my child, about driving around in that luxury car of yours when the streets are so unsafe these days.") But Ilse was devoted to her daughter and when her only remaining child showed up, the rest of the world retreated into the background.

I will always remember, as evidence of her great affection for her mother, a surprise that Alicia prepared for Ilse. When she arrived at Ezeiza airport, Alicia phoned Ilse and asked her to get ready to come down to the lobby of her building in order to help with the luggage. On the arrival of the taxi, Ilse walked up to Alicia's car and saw that her daughter was surrounded by suitcases. Then, suddenly, Andrea's head popped up from among the bags. Ilse had not been expecting to see her youngest granddaughter in Buenos Aires.

ILSE TALKS ABOUT RETURNING TO EUROPE

A very special memory from those days concerns Ilse's decision to move to Spain. It was July 11, 2002, Alicia was in Buenos Aires on one of her frequent trips, and the three of us were having lunch at Los Mirasoles, Alicia's favorite restaurant in Puerto Madero. Over lunch, Alicia told us about a large duplex apartment, quite similar to the one Ilse had in Buenos Aires, that she had bought off-plan some time before in Alcalá de Henares, 30 kilometers northeast of Madrid. She said that construction work would be completed towards the end of the year. Alicia had become a chaired professor (catedrática) at the prestigious University of Alcalá, the second oldest in Spain after Salamanca University, and she wanted to live close to the university where she was teaching. Alcalá de Henares is the birthplace of Miguel de Cervantes, author of *Don Quixote*.

However, before this, in November 2001, Ilse had already told me that she wanted to move to Spain. She also added two important details: When she did go, it would be for good, and it would happen around May or June of the following year. Ilse claimed that it had been her daughter's decision, but Alicia later told me that it was her mother who had made the choice, as she was worried about spending the last years of her life far away from her daughter and grandchildren, whom she wanted near her when the end came.

Doubtless, Ilse was right. It made sense that she should be scared of being alone as the end drew nearer, and in light of the subsequent events, I now accept that decision. However, I also think that Ilse did not want to tell her friends that she had chosen to leave her "family from Argentina" (the Pittalugas and others) and her beloved Buenos Aires. She was pulling up her roots for the third time in her life — first Ölmutz and Prague, then Buenos Aires, and finally Alcalá de Henares — and she wanted to ensure that she did not hurt our feelings.

During the first half of 2002, Ilse began preparing for her definitive journey to Spain. She paid no attention to our endless warnings about the risk of making such a significant change without first trying it out for two or three months, just to get a sense of what life would be like for her there, and above all what life would be like far away from Buenos Aires. It was useless to point out the dangers of burning her bridges and closing off all possibility of return to the Buenos Aires that she loved so much and where she felt so comfortable if the new setting did not agree with her. Ilse had made up her mind to move to Alcalá de Henares to spend her last years there. Alicia agreed entirely with this plan; she was happy that her mother would be near, and was providing her with what she needed to make this great dream a reality: the duplex that she first mentioned over lunch at Los Mirasoles, which would be ready to move into later that year or in early 2003.

The decision had been made. Ilse began sifting through her things – ornaments, clothes, furniture and other belongings. She gave away some, packed what she wanted to keep and shipped it to Spain, threw out the rest, and put her wonderful apartment up for sale. It was a thirteenth-floor property across from the botanical garden, with a splendid balcony that was always filled with flowers, and had incredible views that she enjoyed every day.

Argentina was gripped at the time by a tremendous economic, financial and social crisis known as "the corralito." It was not the right time to sell anything, as things had lost more than half their real value. But Ilse sold it all, from her magnificent apartment to most of her furniture. She sold it at laughable prices. She also gave away clothes, furniture, ornaments and dinnerware sets. Ilse was leaving Argentina for good. She was leaving in order to be reunited with her family. Her acute awareness of the important things in life, even when the rest of us were aware of nothing, told her that she had to go. Her daughter and grandchildren were in Madrid. They would be by her side when she needed them. They would hold her hand, stroke her hair and quench her thirst for affection. She would take the image of them with her when she left this world.

When she sold her apartment, she accepted that the new owners would take possession almost immediately. Her flight was scheduled to coincide with the arrival in Spain of the container with her belongings, which meant that she could not leave immediately, but had to remain in Buenos Aires for five more weeks. A decisive woman to the end, she rented a furnished apartment that was also on the thirteenth floor, had similar views of the botanical garden, and was located less than 30 meters away from her former home. She moved in on November 1 and waited for her departure date. This was the first step in breaking away from her Argentine life. Those last few days were very busy for Ilse: She said goodbye to her friends and put her affairs in order. These last days also afforded her the necessary time to deal emotionally with her own imminent departure.

On November 7, her birthday, I took Ilse and Liliana (her first daughter-in-law, with whom she had always kept in touch) to lunch at Happening, a restaurant in Puerto Madero. On Saturday, November 16, I made the following comments in my journal: "Ilse is sad, very sad." On Thursday, November 21, she went to see her physician, who found her in very good shape. On Wednesday, November 27, she went to the hairdresser at ten in the morning, and at noon she called me in tears. I tried to calm her down and went over to see her. On Thursday, December 5, I rounded up a small group of her closest friends for a farewell party: Marga and Alberto Indij and their children Javier and Andrea; Agie Kupferminc, Mirta Kupferminc and her husband Kurt Frieder, Ivonne Pittaluga, Liliana and Luigi Fiorin, and Diana and Julio Weisberg. Sadly, Edith Silber, whom Ilse had appreciated so much, was unable to attend for health reasons. On Friday, December 13, Ilse said goodbye to Mercedes Güiraldes over the phone. On Sunday, December 15, 2002, Ilse left for Spain.

OPERATION FAREWELL

As a show of our affection, I thought we should surprise Ilse on the day of her departure. I spoke with the Pittalugas and proposed that each of us, separately, should drop by her house to say goodbye, pretending that we would be unable to go to the airport with her. This we did, being careful to take turns presenting her with our various excuses. Ilse was to leave the house a little before seven o'clock in the evening. I was to go to her house at five o'clock and spend no more than 20 minutes there, to give the other conspirators enough time to put on their own performance. We each had an assigned time of arrival and departure, and we all had to stick to the schedule faithfully to ensure that we would have enough time left to drive to Ezeiza, park the cars and regroup inside the airport to surprise Ilse as she walked in.

Everything worked according to plan, and when Ilse arrived she was really happy to see us, and kept thanking us for the big surprise. We took pictures, kept her company until boarding time, and said goodbye, this time for real. She was smiling as she left, waving goodbye with her hand held high and an almost childish look of joy on her face, which somewhat mitigated the sadness of the moment. Once again, Ilse Kaufmann had won. It was getting dark. I was trying not to cry, but the tears kept rolling down my cheeks.

— Helena Pardo

ACKNOWLEDGMENTS

We would like to sincerely thank the people who helped make this book a reality by expressing their interest in the project, providing us with the information and photographic material we needed, or by putting us in touch with the institutions that could do so.

We are especially grateful to Dr. Carlos Sersale, Foreign Affairs Minister of Argentina; Agie Kupferminc for her translations from Hungarian to Spanish; Bedriska Novotná, secretary at the Embassy of the Czech Republic, for her translations from Czech to Spanish; Mr. Podcs, of the firm Prácticos del Río de la Plata S.A., who kindly put us in touch with the National Nautical School; Captain José M. Aldazábal, an instructor at the National Nautical School, who kindly gave us a photograph of the ship *Cabo de Hornos*, as well as information about it and about its twin ship, the *Cabo de Buena Esperanza*, two vessels that are highly relevant to this story; Dorothée Moncayo, who sent us the German text of Gretchen's monologue in *Faust*, which coincided exactly with the passage that Ilse had memorized; Marta Santana, who translated from French into Spanish the notes relating to Alicia Heller's failed trip to Paris, and who also gave us updates on places in Prague mentioned in this book following a recent trip she took there; Paola Ravenna de Colbert, who took time out during her trip to Prague to take pictures of the buildings where Ilse had lived – some of which were used to illustrate this book – and who also provided us with an image of the ship *Cabo de Buena Esperanza*; and Pedro María Martín of the Hotel Carlton in Bilbao and Amaya Mújica of the Basque Museum in Bilbao for the images and references to the Hotel Inglaterra.

Special thanks go to our friends Agie, Marga and Mirta Kupferminc, who were with us from the very beginning.

Ilse and Helena Pardo, 2001.

FINAL THANKS

The book you have in your hands would not have been possible without the perseverance of my mother Alicia. She convinced my grandmother to give the gift of the family story to her grandchildren, and she gave the support my grandmother needed to have the space and support to write the book about her life. She was the one who, coincidentally, met the painter Mirta Kupferminc, and through her she met Mirta's mother, who then introduced my mother to Helena Pardo.

Thanks to my mother, Helena Pardo and my grandmother met and they were able to begin a relationship that would mature and enable Ilse's life to slowly unfold and become written text. During this process of creation it was again my mother who found an editor in Argentina who put those words and pictures into the first edition of my grandmother's story.

My mother was also the person who helped my grandmother leave Argentina when the 2001 crisis began and she supported Ilse on her journey back to Europe, more than 60 years after she had left the continent in 1940.

My mother gave her mother a new home, a new family and a new opportunity to enjoy the last years of her life with her loved ones. After my grandmother's death, my mother again, through her stubbornness, went to Yad Vashem and arranged for this inspiring story to be translated into English, so that more people could read this amazing story, which is worth telling and sharing with the world.

This is a story of never giving up, of fighting for what you believe in and for your life, and of succeeding through adversity without losing hope. This is a story to which my mother has given much of her time and energy in order for this book to become a reality in Spanish and English.

For all of this, thank you Mum!

— Alex Swiec Kaufmann

Ilse with Alicia and her grandchildren, Andrea and Alex, Madrid, 2003.